Wanda E. Brunstetter's

Amish Friends
From Scratch
COOKBOOK

*A Collection of Over 270 Recipes
for Simple Hearty Meals and More*

BARBOUR BOOKS
An Imprint of Barbour Publishing, Inc.

© 2020 by Wanda E. Brunstetter

Print ISBN 978-1-64352-708-6

All scripture quotations are taken from the King James Version of the Bible.

Published by Barbour Books, an imprint of Barbour Publishing, Inc., 1810 Barbour Drive, Uhrichsville, Ohio 44683, www.barbourbooks.com

Our mission is to inspire the world with the life-changing message of the Bible.

Printed in China.

INTRODUCTION

Growing up in a home where most of our meals were made with basic recipes that didn't include prepackaged food, I can relate to how our Amish friends prefer to cook from scratch when possible. Just as my mother, father, and aunts handed down their favorite recipes to me, I have seen our Amish friends do the same with their children and grandchildren.

The Amish mothers I know have taught their children how to cook tasty meals made with fresh ingredients, just as I was taught by my mother and father, who both enjoyed spending time in the kitchen.

My husband and I have benefited from many of the wonderful meals served to us in our Amish friends' homes. I've often returned home with recipes they've graciously shared, such as those found in this cookbook.

Since most Amish live in rural areas and usually have ample space to grow a garden, it's easy for them to get fresh fruits, vegetables, and herbs to include in their meals. Many Amish families raise cows, chickens, turkeys, hogs, and sheep to sell or for their own families to eat. Also available to the Plain people are local butchers, farmers' markets, produce stands, and a variety of auctions where they can purchase home-grown meat, produce, and many types of bulk foods.

I hope you will enjoy the selection of recipes in this cookbook that are made from scratch and served in Amish homes or at their various functions.

Much thanks to my editor, Rebecca Germany, for compiling a good many of the recipes that were submitted by Amish friends.

WANDA E. BRUNSTETTER

He causeth the grass to grow
for the cattle, and herb for
the service of man: that
he may bring forth food
out of the earth.

PSALM 104:14

TABLE of CONTENTS

Finger Licking Good

Grease on the ceiling, splattering from the pan. Dishes scattered everywhere in my small kitchen.

It's a brand-new day and just the beginning!

Breakfast consists of fried potatoes, bacon, eggs, and ancient sourdough toast slathered with slabs of real butter. It melts down into the cracks and oozes out the other side. The fingers catch it from there; it's called "finger licking good!" It just doesn't get much better than that!

Real food. Made in antique cast-iron pans over fifty years old. No premixes. No prepackages. Recapturing the cooking of real food! Today, so many times "easy" is our go-to because of the busyness of our day. My love for authenticity overrides the easy, as I love to recapture the days of authentic foods and know exactly what goes into each dish!

As I wash the dishes, my two-year-old comes up from behind, saying, "Up."

I lift her onto the counter beside me with my pile of dishes. "Clean feet," she says, stretching out her toes. Her idea of washing dishes and cleaning feet is dangling her feet in the water and splashing. "Not today," I tell her. Instead, I give her a bowl of suds from the water, and she proceeds to "wash" everything in sight. As I finish my chore, she holds up her dress and says, "Mess! New dress." Yes, her dress is now wet and requires a change. This is just one of the many dresses we will go through today.

As I go about my day of cooking and cleaning, I make sure she is included every step of the way. There is no better way to teach her that food doesn't just come from a grocery store shelf; instead, it comes from soil, raised from the earth and put there by God for our enjoyment.

Family get-togethers. Church functions. Inviting friends into our home for a meal. All are centered on home-cooked meals. These are some of the things that warm my heart. What better way to enjoy fellowship and friendship as we walk our journey in life?

God bless you, my friends, as you rediscover the love of friendships that bloom and flourish, the charm created with home-cooked meals from scratch!

Betty Troyer, Sarasota, FL

BREAKFAST

Aunt Elma's Buttermilk Pancakes

2 cups flour

3 teaspoons baking powder

½ teaspoon salt

⅓ teaspoon baking soda

2 eggs, well beaten

1¾ cups buttermilk

4 tablespoons vegetable oil

Sift flour, baking powder, salt, and baking soda together in bowl. Add beaten eggs, buttermilk, and oil. Mix well. Drop by spoonfuls on slightly greased hot griddle. When bubbles appear, turn cakes and brown other side. Serve hot with butter and maple syrup. Makes 15 to 18 pancakes depending on size.

Wanda Brunstetter

Pancakes

1½ cups flour
3½ teaspoons baking
  powder
¾ teaspoon salt

3 tablespoons sugar
1 egg, well beaten
3 tablespoons lard, melted
1 cup milk

Sift together flour, baking powder, and salt. Add sugar, egg, lard, and milk. If too thick, thin with a bit more milk. Drop by spoonfuls into greased frying pan and fry both sides.

Mrs. Eli A. Kurtz, Dayton, PA

Fluffy Pancakes

2 cups flour
2 tablespoons sugar
4 teaspoons baking powder
1 teaspoon salt
2 egg yolks

2 cups buttermilk or milk
2 tablespoons butter,
  melted
2 egg whites, beaten stiff

Stir together flour, sugar, baking powder, and salt. Beat egg yolks and add buttermilk and butter. Add to flour mixture. Beat until smooth. Fold in beaten egg whites. Pour ⅓ cup batter for each cake on hot griddle. Cook until bubbles form then flip and cook other side.

Rebecca Swartzentruber, Dalton, OH

Whole Wheat Oatmeal Pancakes

2 eggs
1 cup oats
1 cup whole wheat flour
1½ cups milk
4 tablespoons oil

2 tablespoons sugar or
  honey
6 teaspoons baking powder
½ teaspoon salt

Mix all ingredients. Let sit for a few minutes. If too thick, add a bit more milk. Drop by spoonfuls into greased frying pan. When batter bubbles and edges brown, flip to fry other side.

Mary Petersheim, Apple Creek, OH

CRISPY WAFFLES

2 cups flour
1 tablespoon baking powder
1 teaspoon salt
2 tablespoons sugar

3 eggs, separated
1½ cups milk
½ cup oil

Sift together flour, baking powder, salt, and sugar. Beat together egg yolks, milk, and oil. Stir in dry ingredients. In separate bowl, beat egg whites until stiff and fold into mixture until just moistened. Spray preheated waffle grids with nonstick spray. Ladle 1 cup batter onto grids. Bake according to manufacturer's directions. When done, lift out with fork and serve warm.

MARILYN BONTRAGER, Lagrange, IN

WAFFLES

1½ cups flour
½ teaspoon salt
1 tablespoon sugar
2 teaspoons baking powder

2 eggs, separated
1 cup milk
4 tablespoons butter, melted

Mix flour, salt, sugar, and baking powder. Beat egg yolks into milk. Add to first mixture. Add butter. Beat egg whites until stiff and add to mixture. Spray preheated waffle grids with nonstick spray. Ladle 1 cup batter onto grids. Bake according to manufacturer's directions. When done, lift out with fork and serve warm.

MRS. DAVID J. KURTZ, Smicksburg, PA

Stuffed French Toast

1 loaf homemade bread
2 (8 ounce) packages cream
   cheese
12 eggs
2 cups milk
½ cup maple syrup

Cinnamon (optional)
2 cups fresh or frozen
   berries (optional for
   topping)
Chopped nuts (optional for
   topping)

Cube bread and place half in 9x13-inch pan. Cube cream cheese and sprinkle on top. Add remaining bread cubes. In bowl, beat eggs, milk, and syrup and pour over bread. Sprinkle with cinnamon if desired. Let sit for a while to let bread absorb liquid. Or refrigerate overnight and bake next morning. Bake at 350 degrees for 45 minutes, or until golden brown. Serve with maple syrup. Add fruit or nuts as desired for topping.

SADIE ANNE KAUFFMAN, Gordonville, PA

Baked Oatmeal

2 eggs
½ cup vegetable oil
1 cup sugar
3 cups oats

1 cup milk
2 teaspoons baking powder
Pinch salt

Mix eggs, vegetable oil, and sugar together. Add oats, milk, baking powder, and salt. Stir until well mixed. Pour into 9x13-inch pan and bake at 350 degrees for 30 minutes. Good served warm with fruit and milk.

Elaine Nolt, Ephrata, PA

Granola Cereal

8 to 10 cups quick oats
6 cups crisped rice cereal
2 packages graham
    crackers, coarsely
    crushed
2 teaspoons baking soda
½ teaspoon salt
5 sticks butter
1 cup brown sugar

Mix oats, rice cereal, graham crackers, baking soda, and salt. Melt butter and add brown sugar. Pour over cereal mixture. Bake 2½ hours at 275 degrees, stirring occasionally. This mixture is very wet, which is what makes it so crunchy when it is done. You can also use 1½ cups maple syrup instead of brown sugar.

ROSANNA FISHER, Woodward, PA

Grape Nuts

2½ pounds brown sugar
1 cup butter, softened
1 teaspoon salt
4 pounds whole wheat flour
1 teaspoon maple flavoring
2 tablespoons baking soda
1¼ quarts sour milk or
    buttermilk

Stir all together. Divide into 3 cake pans. Bake at 350 degrees for 30 minutes until brown. Cool. Grind with hand grinder. Toast at 250 degrees for 20 to 30 minutes until crumbs are dry. Serve with milk.

MRS. DAVID J. KURTZ, Smicksburg, PA

French Toast Casserole

1 loaf bread, cubed
1 pound sausage, browned
12 eggs
1 cup maple syrup
2 cups milk
1 (8 ounce) package cream
   cheese, softened

Put bread in 9x13-inch pan. Sprinkle with sausage. In bowl, beat together eggs, maple syrup, and milk. Add cream cheese. Pour over bread. Let sit covered overnight in refrigerator. Bake uncovered at 350 degrees for 1 hour. Serve with maple syrup.

RHODA SCHWARTZ, Monroe, IN

Deluxe Oven-Baked Omelets

6 eggs, beaten
1½ cups milk
½ teaspoon salt
1 teaspoon prepared
   mustard
3 slices bread, cubed
¼ cup chopped onion
1 cup shredded cheese,
   divided
½ pound sausage, browned

Beat together eggs, milk, salt, and mustard. Mix in bread, onion, ½ cup cheese, and sausage. Pour into 9x9-inch pan. Bake at 350 degrees for 35 minutes. Sprinkle with remaining ½ cup cheese. Bake until just melted.

MARTHA BEECHY, Butler, OH

Egg and Potato Casserole

- 6 potatoes, chopped
- 1 medium onion
- 1 cup meat of choice
- 12 eggs
- 1 pint green beans
- 1 cup chopped green pepper
- 2 cups Velveeta cheese

Fry potatoes, onion, and meat together. Put in bottom of casserole dish. Fry eggs, beans, and green pepper. Put on top of potato mixture. Cover with cheese.

White Sauce:

- 3 tablespoons butter
- 2 tablespoons flour
- Milk
- Salt and pepper to taste

In saucepan, brown butter and flour. Add milk, thinning just enough for a rather thick sauce. Season to taste. Pour over cheese layer. Bake at 350 degrees for 20 to 30 minutes until hot through.

William and Rebecca Troyer, Navarre, OH

Simple Cheese Quiche

1 unbaked pie shell
5 large eggs, beaten
1 cup milk
1 cup cream

1 teaspoon salt
1 teaspoon pepper
½ cup bacon bits
1 cup shredded cheese

Bake pie shell for 10 minutes until lightly browned. Beat eggs, milk, cream, salt, and pepper until well blended. Stir in bacon bits and cheese. Carefully pour into warm pie shell. Bake at 350 degrees for 40 to 50 minutes until quiche is light brown. Allow to cool at least 20 minutes before cutting and serving.

Martha Beechy, Butler, OH

Deep-Fried Breakfast Pizza Pockets

Crust:

3 cups flour
1 tablespoon instant yeast
¼ cup vegetable oil

½ teaspoon salt
1 cup warm water

Mix together and roll out thin. Cut into squares.

Filling:

1 (8 ounce) carton sour
  cream
1 can cream of mushroom
  soup
4 medium potatoes,
  chopped and fried
15 eggs, scrambled and
  fried

2 pounds sausage, fried
1 pound diced or shredded
  cheese
Onion, diced
Green pepper, diced
Oil for frying

Mix sour cream and soup. Spread on crust dough, but not to the edge. Layer on a bit of potatoes, egg, sausage, cheese, onion, and green pepper to each square of dough. Fold in half. Press edges closed with fork. Deep-fry in oil until golden brown. Serve warm.

Susie L. Schwartz, Geneva, IN

Quick Fried Mush

2 cups cornmeal
1 teaspoon salt

⅛ cup whole wheat flour
3 cups boiling water

Mix cornmeal, salt, and flour. Add boiling water. Drop by spoonfuls in hot greased skillet. Press flat with spatula. Brown both sides. If batter gets too thick, add a bit of water.

RUBY BONTRAGER, Lagrange, IN

Yogurt Parfait

2½ cups granola
1 (8 ounce) package cream
   cheese, softened
½ cup sour cream

4 cups yogurt
2 tablespoons lemon juice
1 (8 ounce) carton whipped
   topping

Put granola in bottom of 9x13-inch pan. Mix together cream cheese, sour cream, yogurt, lemon juice, and whipped topping. Spread over granola. Top with desired fruit.

SUSAN BONTRAGER, Lagrange, IN

BEVERAGES

Homemade Root Beer

2 cups sugar
1 teaspoon yeast

4 teaspoons root beer extract

Put all ingredients in gallon jar and fill with lukewarm water. Shake until sugar dissolves. Set in sun for 3 to 4 hours. Refrigerate and serve. Hint: don't fill the jar all the way to the top so that it has room to expand.

BARBARA YODER, Gilman, WI

LEAH S. YODER, Glenville, PA

Cappuccino Mix

4 cups powdered milk
2 cups powdered sugar
1⅓ cups chocolate drink
  mix

1½ cups french vanilla
  creamer powder
½ cup instant coffee

Mix together and store in airtight container. Use ¼ cup mix per mug and fill with hot water.

MARILYN BONTRAGER, Lagrange, IN

Hot Chocolate Mix

1 (32 ounce) can creamer
  powder
6 cups (2 pounds) powdered
  sugar

6 cups sugar
2½ cups cocoa powder
2 tablespoons salt

Mix all together in large sealable container. To use, put 3 teaspoons mix in cup and fill with hot water.

CHRIS J.K. SCHWARTZ, Galesburg, KS

Iced Coffee

2 tablespoons instant coffee
¾ cup sugar
2 cups hot water

¾ gallon milk
Ice cubes

Dissolve coffee and sugar in hot water. Add milk and ice. Add more coffee for stronger flavor.

VALERIE BORNTRAGER, Kalona, IA

Tea to Freeze

4 quarts water
4 cups fresh tea leaves
4 cups sugar

Bring water to a boil. Remove from heat and add tea leaves. Let sit 15 minutes. Strain out leaves. Add sugar and cool. Put in containers and freeze. To serve, mix 1 part concentrate to 3 parts water.

MARY PETERSHEIM, Apple Creek, OH

Gelatin Drink

½ cup flavored gelatin
1 cup boiling water

1 liter lemon-lime soda pop

Pour into flat-bottom dish. Chill until firm. Cut gelatin into ½-inch squares. Add several squares gelatin to glass of cold lemon-lime soda pop.

MARTHA SCHMUCKER, Sturgis, MI

Banana Punch

2 cups sugar
3 cups water
⅛ teaspoon salt
6 ounces frozen orange juice
concentrate

1 (46 ounce) can pineapple juice
3 bananas, mashed
2 liters lemon-lime soda pop

In saucepan, combine sugar, water, and salt. Bring to a boil and cook for 10 minutes. Cool down and chill. Add orange juice concentrate, pineapple juice, and bananas. Mix well. Stir in soda pop. Chill.

LENA HOCHSTETLER, Mount Vernon, OH

Mojito Drink Concentrate

2 sprigs mint tea leaves
½ teaspoon sugar
2 to 3 thin lime slices
½ teaspoon sugar
Lemon-lime soda pop

Place mint sprigs and ½ teaspoon sugar in small glass bowl. Use scraper handle and bruise well. Add lime slices and ½ teaspoon sugar to mixture. Muddle together to get plenty of liquid, and let sit a couple of minutes. I usually keep making the concentrate until I have a pint full. It is time consuming but worth it!

Place 3 teaspoons concentrate in glass and fill with soda pop and ice cubes. Looks nice with mint leaves and lime in glass. Garnish glass with lime slice. (May add more concentrate according to your taste.)

LORENE BYLER, Irvington, KY

Orange Punch

1 (46 ounce) can orange juice
1 (46 ounce) can pineapple juice
1 (6 ounce) can frozen orange juice concentrate
1 (6 ounce) can frozen lemonade concentrate
1 package strawberry Kool-Aid
2 cups sugar
2 quarts water
1 quart lemon-lime soda pop

Mix all ingredients except for soda pop. Mixture can be frozen. Thaw partially before serving. Add soda pop when ready to serve.

ROSANNA PETERSHEIM, Junction City, OH

Favorite Punch

1 (12 ounce) can frozen grape juice concentrate
1 (16 ounce) can frozen orange juice concentrate
¼ cup lemon juice
1 cup sugar
1½ cups water
1 to 2 quarts ginger ale or lemon-lime soda pop
Ice cubes

Mix grape and orange juice concentrates. Add lemon juice, sugar, and water. Stir until sugar dissolves. Add ginger ale, ice, and additional water to fill 1-gallon container.

MRS. ENOS (MARIA) WICKEY, Monroe, IN

Mr. Misty Punch

1 (6 ounce) box flavored
  gelatin
1½ cups sugar
1 quart boiling water
1 (14 ounce) can pineapple
  juice

2 quarts water
2 liters lemon-lime soda
  pop

Dissolve gelatin and sugar in boiling water, stirring well. Add pineapple juice and water. Freeze. Before serving, allow frozen punch to thaw a bit. Pour soda pop over top.

Marlene Kay Yoder, Millersburg, IN

Warm Party Punch

4 cups apple juice
48 whole cloves
4 oranges, halved
3 cinnamon sticks

4 cups pineapple juice
2 cups orange juice
3 tablespoons lemon juice
Fresh mint sprigs

Heat apple juice to boiling then turn down heat. Place 6 cloves in each orange half. Drop oranges and cinnamon sticks into apple juice. Steep for 20 minutes. Add pineapple, orange, and lemon juices. Simmer for 30 minutes or more. Strain; serve with sprig of mint. Yield: 2½ quarts.

Barbara Yoder, Gilman, WI

BREADS, ROLLS, AND CRACKERS

French Bread

2 tablespoons yeast	1 teaspoon garlic powder
¼ cup sugar	1 tablespoon Italian
2½ cups warm water	seasoning
2 teaspoons salt	⅓ cup Parmesan cheese
2 tablespoons oil	7 cups flour

Dissolve yeast and sugar in warm water. Mix in salt, oil, garlic powder, Italian seasoning, and cheese. Slowly add flour and knead a few times. Let rise until doubled. Punch down. Let rise until doubled again. Shape into 2 loaves. Bake at 350 degrees for 18 to 20 minutes.

Glen Luella Mast, Topeka, IN

HERMAN STARTER

2 cups flour
2 cups warm water

¼ cup sugar
1 tablespoon yeast

Mix all ingredients and place in glass container. Let stand overnight in warm place, covered but not too tightly. Stir, cover, and refrigerate. Stir again every day. The fifth day, divide Herman in two portions. Set one aside to give to a friend with care instructions, and feed the other portion.

FEED FOR HERMAN:

1 cup flour
½ cup sugar

1 cup milk

Add flour, sugar, and milk to Herman. Refrigerate, covered, and stir every day. On the tenth day you can bake with Herman, or reserve 1 cup Herman and feed it again. Refrigerate, covered, and stir every day to use on day 15.

Note: do not use metal bowls or spoons.

MARTHA BEECHY, Butler, OH

BROWN BREAD

2 cups warm water
2 tablespoons sugar
2 tablespoons yeast
¼ cup honey

2 teaspoons salt
¼ cup vegetable oil
2 cups whole wheat flour
4 cups white bread flour

Combine water, sugar, yeast, honey, and salt. Let sit until foamy. Add oil and flours, a little at a time. Stir well. Knead to a stiff dough. Let rise 1 hour, kneading every 15 minutes. Shape into loaves. Place in pans and let rise. Bake at 350 degrees for 35 to 40 minutes.

MARIE B. SCHLABACH, Smicksburg, PA

Maple Wheat Bread

4 cups warm water
⅔ cup maple syrup
2 tablespoons yeast
⅔ cup olive oil

1½ tablespoons salt
8 to 9 cups whole wheat
  flour

Mix warm water, maple syrup, and yeast together. Let sit 5 minutes, then add olive oil, salt, and flour until the right consistency. Knead 5 minutes. Place in greased bowl and let rise until double in bulk. Punch down and divide into 4 equal parts. Shape into loaves and place in greased pans. Cover and let rise about 45 minutes. Bake at 375 degrees for 30 minutes.

Note: can add ½ cup lecithin granules and ½ cup milled flaxseeds if desired.

Neva Hershberger, Apple Creek, OH

Soft Fluffy Wheat Bread for Mixer

½ cup warm water
1 tablespoon yeast

1 tablespoon sugar

Mix warm water, yeast, and sugar in small bowl. Set aside for 10 minutes.

½ teaspoon salt
¼ cup sugar
1 cup warm water
¼ cup lard

1 egg
2 cups whole wheat flour
3 cups bread flour

In mixer bowl, combine salt, sugar, warm water, lard, and egg. Add yeast mixture. Mix briefly. Add whole wheat flour; mix well. Add bread flour as needed. Mix on low speed until combined. Let rise 30 minutes. With dough hook, knead for a few minutes. Let rise again until doubled. Shape into 2 loaves. Pour in greased pans and let rise. Bake at 350 degrees for 25 minutes or until loaves sound hollow when tapped.

Mary Joyce Petersheim, Fredericktown, OH

Hillbilly Bread

4 cups warm water
1 cup brown sugar
3 tablespoons yeast
4 cups whole wheat flour
6 teaspoons salt

1 cup warm water
1 cup oil
3½ pounds (10 to 11 cups) white flour

Mix 4 cups warm water with brown sugar, yeast, whole wheat flour, and salt. Let stand 1 hour. Add 1 cup warm water and oil. Work in white flour until dough is well mixed. Grease large bowl and place dough inside, coating with oil. Cover. Let rise 30 minutes. Knead dough. Let rise again for 1 hour. Put into bread pans. Let rise until doubled. Bake at 350 degrees for 30 minutes.

"Our favorite bread. It stays nice and soft."

RUBY BONTRAGER, Lagrange, IN

Mom's Dinner Rolls

1 cup milk
½ cup maple syrup
½ cup butter
1 tablespoon salt
2 tablespoons yeast

½ cup warm water
3 eggs, beaten
2 cups or more whole wheat
flour

Heat milk until scalding. Add maple syrup, butter, and salt. Dissolve yeast in warm water. Mix milk mixture, eggs, and a little of the flour. Add yeast, being sure milk is not too hot. Add enough flour to make a smooth dough. Let rise until doubled. Knead down and let rise again. Form into buns. Let rise about 30 minutes. Bake at 350 degrees for 25 to 30 minutes until golden brown.

LINDA BURKHOLDER, Fresno, OH

Hamburger Buns

3½ cups warm water
1 cup oil
6 tablespoons yeast
3 eggs, beaten

1 teaspoon salt
½ cup honey
10½ cups flour (part whole
wheat is good)

Mix water, oil, yeast, eggs, salt, and honey, and let sit for 15 minutes. Add flour. Mix well. Shape into buns immediately by rolling out to ½-inch thick and using wide mouth jar ring to cut dough into circles. Place on greased sheets with a little space between buns. Let rise until doubled and bake at 425 degrees for 10 minutes.

These freeze well. For herb buns, add 1 tablespoon garlic powder, 1 tablespoon basil, and 1 tablespoon parsley flakes.

ESTHER PEACHEY, Fleminsburg, KY

Potato Sourdough Buns

STARTER:

1½ cups warm water
1 teaspoon instant yeast
1 cup flour

12 ounces potatoes, cooked
and mashed

Combine water and yeast. Add flour and potatoes. Loosely cover and allow to sit at room temperature for at least 8 hours or up to 24 hours before proceeding.

½ cup warm water
1 egg
2 tablespoons sugar

1 scant tablespoon salt
4 to 4½ cups flour

In bowl, combine starter with water, egg, sugar, salt, and flour using a wooden spoon. Dough should be very soft and slightly sticky. If needed, add a little more flour. Knead 5 minutes. Let rise until doubled. Form balls and flatten. Let rise 45 minutes. Bake at 350 degrees for 15 to 20 minutes.

MARIE B. SCHLABACH, Smicksburg, PA

CROISSANT ROLLS

1 cup butter
⅓ cup flour
1½ cups warm water
1 tablespoon yeast
1 teaspoon salt
3 tablespoons brown sugar
2½ tablespoons potato flakes

⅓ cup dry milk
⅓ cup cornstarch
3 cups flour
1 egg
1 tablespoon milk
Sugar

Cut together butter and ⅓ cup flour. Place on waxed paper. Fold over paper and press or roll into 10x4-inch rectangle. Chill 1 hour, no longer.

Stir together warm water and yeast. Let sit to dissolve. Mix salt, brown sugar, potato flakes, dry milk, cornstarch, and 3 cups flour into yeast mixture. Mix to soft dough. Knead lightly. Place in oiled bowl. Cover and let rise 1 hour.

On floured surface, roll yeast dough into 12-inch square. Place chilled mixture on center of square. Fold sides over chilled mixture. Roll into 12-inch square. Repeat the fold and roll three more times. Place in covered bowl and chill 1 hour.

Divide dough in half. Roll each half into 12-inch circle. Cut each circle into 8 to 12 wedges. Roll up from widest edge to point. Place on greased baking sheets. Let rise 1 hour.

Mix egg and milk. Brush tops of rolls and sprinkle with sugar. Bake at 375 degrees for 15 to 20 minutes until golden brown.

KATHRYN TROYER, Rutherford, TN

Aunt Elma's Buttermilk Corn Bread

½ cup flour
3 teaspoons baking powder
1 teaspoon salt
¼ teaspoon baking soda
1 teaspoon sugar

1½ cups white cornmeal
1 egg (optional)
1½ cups buttermilk
4 tablespoons shortening, melted

Sift flour, baking powder, salt, baking soda, and sugar into bowl. Add cornmeal. In another bowl, beat egg and milk then add to dry mixture to make a stiff batter. Add shortening. Beat until well mixed. Poor into greased shallow pan. Bake at 425 degrees for about 25 minutes. Break or cut into pieces; serve with butter.

Wanda Brunstetter

Apple Muffins

2¼ cups flour
1 tablespoon baking powder
½ teaspoon salt
1½ teaspoons cinnamon
½ cup sugar

1 egg, beaten
⅔ cup milk
½ cup vegetable oil
1½ cups apple chunks
Cinnamon-sugar mixture

In large bowl, combine flour, baking powder, salt, cinnamon, and sugar. In another bowl, combine egg, milk, and oil. Stir into first mixture until all is just moistened. Stir in apples. Spoon into muffin pans, filling each cup three-quarters full. Sprinkle cinnamon-sugar mixture on top. Bake at 400 degrees for 20 to 25 minutes.

ELLEN BRENNEMAN, Danville, AL

BANANA BREAD

3 very ripe bananas,
  mashed
1 cup sugar
½ teaspoon salt
1 teaspoon baking soda

½ cup oil
½ cup milk
2 cups flour
½ cup chopped nuts
Raisins (optional)

Mix all ingredients together. Divide into 2 bread pans and bake at 350 degrees for about 1 hour.

MARTHA BEECHY, Butler, OH

ZUCCHINI BREAD

4 cups flour
1 teaspoon baking soda
1 teaspoon salt
½ teaspoon baking powder
2 teaspoons cinnamon
½ teaspoon nutmeg
¼ teaspoon cloves

3 eggs, beaten
1 cup oil
2 cups brown sugar
3 teaspoons vanilla
3 cups shredded zucchini
1 cup chopped nuts

Mix all ingredients well and put in 3 or 4 greased bread pans. Bake at 350 degrees for 1 hour. You could serve plain or frosted with caramel icing.

MARTHA BEECHY, Butler, OH

BAKED DOUGHNUTS

1 tablespoon yeast
3 tablespoons sugar
2 cups warm water

3 cups doughnut mix
2 cups flour

Mix yeast and sugar; add water and stir well. Add doughnut mix and flour; mix well. Cover and let rise. Roll out to ½-inch thick. Cut with jar ring or other round cutter. Let rise on cookie sheet. Bake at 350 degrees for 20 minutes or until golden brown. Cool. Cut in half. Spread filling between each half.

FILLING:

2 (3 ounce) boxes instant
vanilla pudding mix
3 cups milk

1 (8 ounce) package cream
cheese, softened

In bowl, mix pudding and milk. In another bowl, beat cream cheese until smooth. Beat in pudding a little at a time.

Notes: You can glaze the doughnuts if you wish. Add some whipped topping to the filling if it is too dense for you. Doughnuts also good with fruit filling and vanilla frosting.

MRS. REUBEN (MARTHA) BYLER, Atlantic, PA

Doughnut Muffins

3 cups flour
1 cup sugar
1 cup brown sugar
2 teaspoons baking powder
1 teaspoon baking soda
½ teaspoon salt
1½ teaspoons cinnamon
½ teaspoon nutmeg
2 eggs
1½ cups apple cider
1 teaspoon vanilla

Combine flour, sugar, brown sugar, baking powder, baking soda, salt, cinnamon, and nutmeg. In small bowl, blend eggs, apple cider, and vanilla. Add to dry mixture until just moistened. Fill greased muffin cups two-thirds full. Bake at 350 degrees for 20 to 25 minutes.

Topping:

¾ cup butter, melted
1½ cups sugar
3½ teaspoons cinnamon

Coat each warm muffin with butter. Combine sugar and cinnamon. Roll buttered muffins in mixture.

Dorcas Marie Yoder, Meyersdale, PA

Sweet Dough Doughnuts

1 quart milk
2 sticks margarine
3 tablespoons yeast
1 cup lukewarm water
1 cup sugar

4 eggs, beaten
1 teaspoon salt
12 cups flour (approx.)
Lard for frying

In saucepan, scald milk and add margarine. Set aside to cool. In large bowl, combine yeast, water, and sugar. After yeast is dissolved, add beaten eggs and cooled milk. Add salt and enough flour to have a soft and handleable dough. Let rise until doubled in size. Roll out and cut. Let rise again. Fry in lard until golden brown. Yield: about 4 dozen depending on size.

Cream Filling:

1 (8 ounce) package cream
cheese

¼ cup margarine
2 cups powdered sugar

Cream together cream cheese and margarine. Beat in powdered sugar. Beat until smooth.

Doughnut Glaze:

1 pound powdered sugar
1 tablespoon Perma-Flo

2 teaspoons vanilla
Water

Mix powdered sugar and Perma-Flo. Add vanilla and just enough water to make a glaze that is not too thin.

MRS. MONROE (ALMA) BORNTRAGER, Glasgow, KY

CRÈME-FILLED DOUGHNUT BARS

2 tablespoons yeast
1 cup warm water
¼ cup sugar
¼ cup vegetable oil

1 teaspoon salt
1 egg, beaten
½ cup doughnut mix
3½ cups flour

Dissolve yeast in water. Add sugar, oil, and salt. Mix in egg. Add doughnut mix and flour. Mix dough well and let rise until doubled. Roll out dough onto cookie sheet. Let rise again. Bake at 350 degrees for 15 to 20 minutes. When cooled, cut in half horizontally.

FILLING:

1 cup scalded milk, cooled
½ cup instant vanilla
    pudding mix

1 (8 ounce) package cream
    cheese
1 (8 ounce) carton whipped
    topping

Combine filling ingredients until smooth and spread between layers.

FROSTING:

½ cup butter
1 cup brown sugar
½ cup milk

2 cups or more powdered
    sugar
Cinnamon-sugar mixture

In saucepan, melt butter, add brown sugar, and boil for 2 minutes, stirring constantly. Add milk and continue stirring until mixture comes to a boil. When cooled, add powdered sugar. Spread on top of bars and sprinkle with cinnamon-sugar mixture.

LOVINA BYLER, Brockway, PA

Maple Twists

¼ cup warm water
¾ cup warm milk
⅓ cup margarine
1 teaspoon salt

¼ cup sugar
2 eggs, beaten
3 to 4 cups flour
2 tablespoons instant yeast

Mix water, milk, margarine, salt, sugar, and eggs. Add flour and yeast. Mix well into a soft dough. Let rise then divide into 3 parts. Roll out each portion of dough to fit 12-inch round pizza pan. Lay first layer on pan and sprinkle with filling. Top with second portion of dough and more filling. Repeat for third layer. Set glass down on center of dough circle. Cut dough into 16 wedges, being careful not to cut through center mark. Twist each wedge three times. Let rise. Bake at 350 degrees for 30 minutes. Drizzle with icing.

FILLING:

⅔ cup chopped nuts
⅓ cup sugar
1 teaspoon cinnamon

1½ teaspoons maple flavoring

Mix all well.

ICING:

1½ cups powdered sugar
3 tablespoons milk

Maple flavoring

Mix ingredients until smooth and spreadable.

ELLEN BRENNEMAN, Danville, AL

Cinnamon Rolls

4 packages yeast
1 cup lukewarm water
4 eggs
1½ cups sugar
4½ teaspoons salt
4 cups lukewarm milk

1 stick margarine
¾ cup oil
15 cups flour
Brown sugar
Cinnamon

Dissolve yeast in water. Let sit while you mix eggs, sugar, salt, milk, and margarine. Add yeast and oil. Add flour, a little less or more than 15 cups, until dough handles well. Set in a warm place, covered, to rise until doubled in size. Punch down and let rise again. Roll out. Sprinkle with mixture of brown sugar and cinnamon. Roll dough up and slice. Bake at 350 degrees for 30 minutes until nice and golden brown.

Ruby Bontrager, Lagrange, IN

Overnight Rolls

1 cup boiling water
½ cup sugar
½ cup butter
½ teaspoon salt
½ teaspoon sugar
2 tablespoons warm water

1 package yeast
2 eggs, beaten
4 cups flour, divided
Melted butter
Brown sugar
Cinnamon

Mix boiling water, ½ cup sugar, butter, and salt. Cool to lukewarm. Mix ½ teaspoon sugar, warm water, and yeast, stirring to dissolve. Add to first mixture. Add eggs. Stir in 2 cups flour; beat 3 minutes. Add remaining flour and beat. Refrigerate dough until cold. Roll out dough to ½-inch thick rectangle. Brush with melted butter. Combine brown sugar and cinnamon and sprinkle over dough. Roll up dough and slice. Place in greased pan. Let sit in fridge overnight. In the morning, bake at 375 degrees for 15 minutes. Good with glaze on top.

Betty Miller, Decatur, IN

Sticky Quicky Buns

1½ cups flour
1¾ tablespoons yeast
¾ cup milk
¼ cup butter
¼ cup sugar

⅔ cup water
1 teaspoon salt
1 egg, beaten
1½ cups flour

In large bowl, combine 1½ cups flour and yeast. In saucepan, heat milk and butter. Add sugar, water, and salt, heating until warm. Pour into yeast mixture. Add egg and beat well into mixture. Add 1½ cups flour. Mix well. Let rise for 30 minutes.

Topping:

½ cup butter
1 cup brown sugar
1 teaspoon cinnamon

⅓ cup chopped pecans
1 tablespoon corn syrup
1 tablespoon water

Combine topping ingredients in saucepan; heat until melted. Pour into 9x13-inch pan. Stir down dough and drop by tablespoonfuls onto topping. Bake at 350 degrees for 15 to 20 minutes. When done, flip onto baking sheet so topping is on top. Best served warm.

Crystal Ropp, Kalona, IA

Raspberry Cream Rolls

Dough:

1 cup milk at 70 to 80
   degrees
¼ cup water
1 tablespoon sugar
1 tablespoon yeast
¼ cup butter, softened

1 egg
1 teaspoon salt
¼ cup instant vanilla
   pudding mix
4 cups bread flour, divided

Mix milk, water, sugar, and yeast; set aside. In mixing bowl, mix butter, egg, salt, and pudding mix. Combine with first mixture. Gradually add 2 cups flour at a time. Roll out half of dough. Slice and cut into small pieces. Put pieces into greased 9x13-inch pan, covering bottom.

Filling:

1 egg
⅓ cup sugar
1 (8 ounce) package cream
   cheese, softened

1 (16 ounce) can raspberry
   pie filling

In bowl, mix egg, sugar, and cream cheese. Spread over dough. Spread pie filling over cream cheese mixture. Roll out remaining half of dough, slice, and cut into pieces. Place dough on top of filling. Cover and let rise for 1 hour. Uncover and bake at 350 degrees for 25 minutes or until done. Let rolls cool before icing.

Icing:

4 ounces cream cheese,
   softened
1½ cups powdered sugar

½ teaspoon vanilla
¼ cup butter
1½ teaspoons milk

Blend all ingredients until smooth. Spread over rolls. Cut into squares.

David L. Byler, New Wilmington, PA

Flour Tortillas

2 cups flour
2 teaspoons baking powder
1 teaspoon salt

¼ cup shortening or lard
½ cup lukewarm water

Combine flour, baking powder, and salt. Mix in shortening until crumbly. Gradually add water. Form into ball and knead thoroughly until smooth. Divide into 6 balls. Roll each ball out as thin as possible. Drop on very hot ungreased griddle. Flip them every couple of seconds until done. Store in plastic bag or container to keep soft. Use them for your favorite burrito and enchilada casseroles or other recipes.

MARTHA PETERSHEIM, Junction City, OH

Best Pizza Dough

¾ tablespoon yeast
1 cup warm water
1 tablespoon sugar
1 tablespoon vegetable oil

3 cups flour
1 teaspoon garlic salt
1½ teaspoons oregano

Dissolve yeast in water. Add sugar and oil. Add flour, garlic salt, and oregano. Mix well, adding more flour until dough is just no longer sticky. Bake at 450 degrees for 10 to 15 minutes until golden brown, then add your choice of sauce and toppings and bake again until cheese is melted. Yield: 1 large round pizza or 1 jelly roll pan.

KATIE FISHER, Kirkwood, PA

Italian Cheese Bread

1 cup warm water
1 tablespoon vegetable oil
1 tablespoon yeast

1 teaspoon sugar
1 teaspoon salt
2½ cups flour

Mix water, vegetable oil, yeast, sugar, and salt. Add flour and knead until smooth and elastic. Put in greased bowl and let rise for 20 minutes. Punch dough down and spread out on 12-inch pizza pan.

Toppings:

¼ cup Italian dressing
¼ teaspoon garlic salt
¼ teaspoon oregano
¼ teaspoon thyme

⅛ teaspoon pepper
½ cup shredded mozzarella cheese

Combine dressing, garlic salt, oregano, thyme, and pepper, and drizzle on top of dough. Bake at 450 degrees for 15 minutes. Sprinkle cheese on top and let melt in oven. Serve hot.

VALERIE BORNTRAGER, Kalona, IA

"Pizza Hut" Breadsticks

1½ cups warm water
1 tablespoon yeast
1 tablespoon sugar
1¼ teaspoons salt
¼ cup oil
4 cups bread flour

¾ cup butter
1 teaspoon garlic salt
1 tablespoon parsley
1 tablespoon Italian seasoning
Parmesan cheese

Combine water and yeast; dissolve. Add sugar, salt, oil, and flour. Let rise until doubled. Roll out. Cut into 1-inch strips. Place on cookie sheet. In saucepan, melt butter; add garlic salt, parsley, and Italian seasoning. Spread over dough sticks. Let rise slightly. Bake at 350 degrees for 10 to 15 minutes. Sprinkle with Parmesan cheese while still hot. Yield: 50 sticks.

LOVINA NISSLEY, Chatham, VA

Homemade Graham Crackers

2 cups brown sugar
1 cup lard or ¾ cup lard and
¼ cup butter
4 cups graham flour
1 cup flour

1 teaspoon baking soda
1 teaspoon baking powder
1 teaspoon salt
1 cup milk
1 teaspoon vanilla

Cream brown sugar and lard. Sift together graham flour, flour, baking soda, baking powder, and salt. Add to creamed mixture. Dough will be crumbly. Add milk and vanilla. Dough will be sticky and soft. Wrap dough in plastic and chill for about 1 hour. On floured surface, roll out thin and cut into squares. Prick dough with fork. Bake at 350 degrees for 10 to 12 minutes, or until browned but still soft. Store in airtight container.

MARTHA PETERSHEIM, Junction City, OH

Soft Pretzels

½ tablespoon yeast
½ cup warm water
1 tablespoon oil
2 tablespoons brown sugar

½ teaspoon salt
1½ cups flour
Butter, melted
Coarse salt

In bowl, dissolve yeast in warm water with oil and brown sugar until bubbly. Add salt and flour, mixing until smooth. Knead for 5 minutes until smooth and elastic. Let rise for 30 minutes in warm place. Punch down and divide into 5 pieces. Roll each piece into a rope and twist to shape pretzel. Bake on sheet at 350 degrees for 20 to 25 minutes until golden brown. Remove to rack to cool. Brush with melted butter. Sprinkle with coarse salt.

JOANN MILLER, Mount Vernon, OH

Hard Pretzels

Sourdough:

½ teaspoon yeast   ½ cup warm water
½ cup flour

The day before, mix yeast, flour, and warm water. Cover and set on countertop.

Dough:

3 cups warm water   ¼ cup lard
¾ tablespoon yeast   3 teaspoons salt
6 tablespoons sugar   3½ to 4½ cups pastry flour
6 tablespoons brown sugar   3 quarts water
1 tablespoon apple cider   3 tablespoons baking soda
   vinegar   Pretzel salt
5 tablespoons butter

Next day, add warm water, yeast, sugar, brown sugar, vinegar, butter, lard, salt, and flour to sourdough mix. Mix dough, which should be very stiff. Let rise for 1 to 2 hours if not using instant yeast. Punch down, roll out to ¼ to ½ inch thick, and shape into pretzels or sticks. Bring 3 quarts water to a boil and add baking soda. Use big spoon with holes and dip pretzels in boiling soda water one at a time. Place on greased baking sheets. Sprinkle with pretzel salt and bake at 425 degrees until golden. Cool oven to 170 to 200 degrees and put pretzels back in oven to dry. Leave door slightly open. Drying time takes about 6 to 9 hours. They are done when they break easily when twisted slightly.

Serving suggestion: Break into pieces and mix with melted bacon grease or butter and cheddar cheese powder until pretzels are coated. Bake at 200 degrees for 30 minutes, stirring every 10 minutes.

Elizabeth Byler, Milton, PA

Salads and
Side Dishes

Broccoli Salad

3 small heads broccoli
1 head cauliflower
8 slices bacon, fried and
crumbled

Chopped onion
2 cups grated cheese

Dressing:

¾ cup sour cream
¾ cup Miracle Whip salad
dressing

⅓ cup sugar
Dash salt

Cut up broccoli and cauliflower quite fine. Add cooked bacon and chopped onions. Mix dressing ingredients. Add cheese and dressing just before serving.

Ruth Girod, Monroe, IN

Corn Bread Salad

Corn Bread:

½ cup butter
½ cup brown sugar
1 egg, beaten
1 cup milk or buttermilk

1 cup flour
1 cup cornmeal
1 teaspoon baking soda
½ teaspoon salt

Mix butter, brown sugar, and egg. Add milk. Add flour, cornmeal, baking soda, and salt. Pour into greased 9x13-inch pan. Bake at 400 degrees for 20 to 30 minutes.

Dressing:

1½ cups mayonnaise
1 package ranch dressing
    mix

1½ cups sour cream

Mix together.

Salad:

1½ cups pinto beans, rinsed
    and drained
1½ cups corn, drained
¼ cup chopped onion

½ cup chopped green
    pepper
1 cup crumbled fried bacon
1 cup shredded cheese
Chopped tomato

In 9x13-inch pan, crumble corn bread. Spread dressing on top. Layer on beans, corn, onion, green pepper, bacon, and cheese. Refrigerate. Just before serving, top with tomato.

Mrs. Paul Schrock, Salem, MO

Potato Salad

12 cups cooked and
  shredded potatoes
12 eggs, boiled and mashed
½ onion, chopped
2 cups diced celery
1 cup shredded carrots

2 cups mayonnaise
2½ cups sugar
2 teaspoons salt
6 tablespoons yellow
  mustard
¼ cup vinegar

Mix all together. Makes about 1 gallon.

ESTHER BURKHOLDER, Sugarcreek, OH

Ramen Noodle Salad

2 packages ramen noodles
1 bag coleslaw (shredded
  cabbage & carrots)

1 small bunch green onions,
  chopped
1 cup sunflower seeds

Cook ramen noodles in boiling water for 3 minutes. Cool. Add coleslaw, onions, and seeds.

Dressing:

½ cup sugar
½ cup vinegar
½ cup canola oil

2 packages ramen noodle
  chicken flavor

In saucepan, mix sugar and vinegar over low heat until sugar dissolves. Remove from heat and chill. Add oil and chicken flavoring. Add dressing to noodle mixture 1 to 2 hours before serving.

ROSANNA PETERSHEIM, Junction City, OH

Grape Salad

4 pounds seedless grapes
1 (8 ounce) package cream cheese
1 (8 ounce) carton sour cream

1 (8 ounce) carton whipped topping
1½ cups powdered sugar
1 teaspoon lemon juice

Wash and drain grapes well. Mix cream cheese, sour cream, whipped topping, powdered sugar, and lemon juice. Fold in grapes and mix to coat well.

"I also like to add fresh sliced strawberries and pineapple chunks."

MARY SCHWARTZ, Berne, IN

Taco Salad

1 pound ground beef
1 medium onion, diced
1 package taco seasoning
1 head lettuce, torn or chopped
1 large tomato, diced

1 can kidney beans, drained and rinsed
8 ounces cheddar cheese, shredded
1 package nacho-flavored chips, crushed

Brown beef and onion. Reserve 1 tablespoon taco seasoning for dressing and add rest to beef. In large bowl, combine lettuce, tomato, beans, and cheese. When ready to serve, coat with dressing and stir in chips

DRESSING:

1 cup mayonnaise
¼ cup ketchup
1 tablespoon yellow mustard
¼ teaspoon salt
¼ cup oil

¼ cup sugar
2 tablespoons vinegar
½ teaspoon paprika
2 tablespoons water
1 tablespoon taco seasoning

Mix all together.

LIZZIE YODER, Fredericksburg, OH

VEGETABLE PIZZA

CRUST:

1 tablespoon yeast	4 pinches salt
¼ cup sugar	1 egg
2 cups flour	6 tablespoons butter

Combine all ingredients and spread on baking sheet. Bake at 400 degrees for 15 to 20 minutes. Cool.

DRESSING:

1 (8 ounce) package cream cheese	¾ cup mayonnaise
	1 tablespoon ranch dressing

Blend all ingredients until smooth. Spread over crust.

TOPPINGS:

3 cups chopped tomatoes	2 cups shredded cheese
2 cups finely chopped cauliflower	2 cups shredded carrots
	1 cup finely chopped celery

Sprinkle toppings over dressing. Chill.

KATIE E. STOLTZFUS, Charlotte Court House, VA

10-MINUTE NOODLE DOUGH

2 cups egg yolks	3¼ pounds flour
1½ cups boiling water	

Beat together egg yolks and boiling water. Pour yolks over flour and mix. Cover and let sit for 10 minutes. Lightly flour countertop and knead dough until smooth. Roll out thin and cut into strips.

MARTHA SCHMUCKER, Sturgis, MI

Noodles

3 cups egg yolks **4½ pounds flour**
2 cups water

Beat egg yolks with water. Add flour and mix with spoon as long as possible. Then knead with hands. Roll out very thin and cut in strips or run through pasta machine. Spread out to dry.

To cook: Bring half a pot of chicken broth to a boil. Add noodles. Cook 8 to 12 minutes until noodles are tender.

Barbara Yoder, Gilman, WI

CHICKEN DRESSING

2 cups water
1 pint finely chopped celery
1 cup finely chopped carrots
1 cup chicken fat or butter
1 teaspoon salt
¾ teaspoon garlic salt
1¾ tablespoons poultry
  seasoning

1¾ tablespoons chicken
  base
6 quarts breadcrumbs,
  lightly toasted
2½ quarts chicken broth
7 eggs, well beaten
2 quarts cooked chicken

In 2-quart saucepan, bring water, celery, and carrots to a hard boil. Turn off heat and let sit 10 minutes or until carrots are just tender. Add fat to melt. Cool slightly. Add salt, garlic salt, poultry seasoning, and chicken base. Put breadcrumbs in large bowl and mix with broth. Add eggs. Add vegetable mixture. Mix well. Gently add chicken. Put in roaster and refrigerate overnight. When ready to bake, lightly mix to incorporate liquid that may have settled to bottom. Bake at 350 degrees for 1½ to 2 hours. Yield: 1½ to 2 gallons.

ESTHER L. MILLER, Fredericktown, OH

Good Baked Beans

2 quarts cooked navy beans
2 cups brown sugar
¼ cup water
2 teaspoons salt
2 teaspoons onion salt
2 teaspoons liquid smoke
4 tablespoons minced onion
2 tablespoons butter
6 tablespoons bacon grease
1 quart crumbled fried bacon

Mix everything together. Bake at 375 degrees for 1 hour or cook in slow cooker on high heat for 4 to 5 hours.

Mrs. Reuben (Martha) Byler, Atlantic, PA

Green Bean Casserole

¼ cup butter
¼ cup flour
1 cup milk
2 quarts green beans, cooked

Melt butter in saucepan. Gradually add flour. Slowly stir in milk and cook until thickened. Mix in green beans and pour into casserole dish.

Topping:

¼ cup butter
½ teaspoon onion salt
1 cup shredded white American cheese
1 cup breadcrumbs
¼ teaspoon pepper

In saucepan, melt butter. Add onion salt, cheese, breadcrumbs, and pepper. Sprinkle over green beans. Bake at 350 degrees for 25 to 30 minutes.

Elaine Nolt, Ephrata, PA

BAKED FRENCH FRIES

12 potatoes, peeled
2 tablespoons oil

2 teaspoons seasoning

Slice potatoes julienne style. Soak in cold water for 15 minutes to 1 hour. Dry thoroughly by spreading on clean towel and rolling up towel. Dump potatoes in large bowl. Toss with oil and seasonings of your choice. Spread single layer on several greased baking sheets. Bake at 450 degrees for 50 minutes, stirring frequently and rotating pans. Serve with sour cream or salsa.

SUSAN C. SCHWARTZ, Berne, IN

BACON FRIES

½ cup butter
2 cups milk
2 pounds Velveeta cheese
Salt and pepper to taste

French fries, deep-fried or baked
Bacon, fried and crumbled

In saucepan, brown butter. Add milk and bring to a boil. Add cheese, stirring until melted. Season to taste. Spread fries on platter. Pour sauce over and sprinkle generously with bacon. Serve hot.

AMANDA BYLER, Curwensville, PA

SOUR CREAM AND ONION FRIES

2 tablespoons vegetable oil
5 cups potato wedges

1 tablespoon sour cream and onion powder

On sheet pan, pour oil over potatoes. Sprinkle with sour cream and onion powder. Toss to coat. Bake at 350 degrees for 1 hour, turning at least once.

JUDY ZIMMERMAN, East Earl, PA

Garlic Potatoes

3 teaspoons salt

1 teaspoon garlic powder
(or use fresh crushed
garlic)

2 tablespoons minced or
crushed parsley

½ teaspoon pepper

½ teaspoon paprika

1 cup melted butter

4 quarts diced potatoes

Mix seasonings with melted butter and pour over potatoes. Stir until potatoes are well covered and pour into baking dish. Cover baking dish tightly with foil. Bake at 350 degrees for 1½ hours.

Betty Troyer, Sarasota, FL

Potluck Potato Casserole

2 pounds potatoes
¼ cup melted butter
1 pint cream
1 can cream of chicken soup
1 teaspoon salt
¼ teaspoon pepper

½ cup chopped onion
2 cups shredded sharp
cheddar cheese
2 cups crushed cornflakes
¼ cup melted butter

Boil potatoes in skins, peel, and chop. In large bowl, mix potatoes, ¼ cup melted butter, cream, soup, salt, pepper, onion, and cheese. Pour into greased 9x13-inch casserole dish. In bowl, combine cornflakes and ¼ cup melted butter. Spread on top of potatoes. Bake at 350 degrees for 30 minutes until hot through.

RHODA MILLER, Decatur, IN

Potato Pancakes

4 medium baking potatoes
4 eggs, beaten
¼ cup finely chopped onion
¼ cup flour
1 teaspoon salt
¼ cup vegetable oil

Shred potatoes to measure 4 cups. Rinse well, drain, and pat dry. In large bowl, mix potatoes, eggs, onion, flour, and salt. In 12-inch skillet, heat 2 tablespoons oil over medium heat. Measure ¼ cup potato mixture per pancake and flatten into skillet with spatula. Cook about 2 minutes on each side until lightly browned.

Susan C. Schwartz, Berne, IN

Spicy Sweet Potato Fries

3 medium sweet potatoes,
   peeled and cut into strips
2 tablespoons olive oil
2 tablespoons brown sugar
1 tablespoon chili powder
½ teaspoon salt
¼ teaspoon red pepper

Put potatoes in gallon zipper bag. Add olive oil and toss until coated. In bowl, combine brown sugar, chili powder, salt, and red pepper. Add to potatoes in bag and toss to coat. Spread on cookie sheet and bake at 400 degrees for 30 minutes, stir halfway through.

Mabel Yoder, Mount Vernon, OH

CRUNCHY ONION RINGS

1 cup flour
1 teaspoon baking powder
1 teaspoon salt
½ teaspoon seasoned salt

1 egg
¾ cup milk
1 tablespoon oil
2 large onions

Combine flour, baking powder, salt, and seasoned salt. Beat egg, add milk and oil, and stir in flour mixture. Cut onions in ¼-inch rings. Separate rings and dip in batter, one at a time. Drain briefly then drop into hot oil, about 375 degrees. Fry until golden brown; flip and continue to fry other side. Place on paper towel–lined platter and enjoy! These are a hit at our house.

MARTHA BEECHY, Butler, OH

ZUCCHINI BOATS

1 medium zucchini
¼ cup water
⅛ teaspoon salt
1 tablespoon butter or margarine

¼ cup soft breadcrumbs
2 tablespoons chopped stuffed green olives
2 tablespoons shredded cheddar cheese

Cut zucchini in half lengthwise. Scoop out and reserve pulp, leaving ¼-inch shells. Place zucchini shells cut side down in skillet. Add water and bring to a boil. Reduce heat, cover, and simmer for 5 to 6 minutes until tender; drain. Turn shells cut side up on plate. Sprinkle with salt. Chop zucchini pulp and sauté in butter for 5 minutes until tender. Stir in breadcrumbs and olives. Spoon into zucchini shells. Sprinkle with cheddar cheese. Place in skillet, cover, and cook over medium heat (no added water) for 5 minutes or until cheese is melted. Yield: 2 servings.

LENA YODER, McClure, PA

Zucchini Fritters

3 cups grated zucchini
2 eggs
2 tablespoons flour
½ teaspoon salt

1 medium onion, chopped fine, or ½ teaspoon garlic powder
½ cup grated cheese (optional)

Mix well. Drop by tablespoonfuls onto well-greased skillet on medium heat. Fry until golden brown; turn and fry other side. Delicious on sandwiches with tomatoes, onions, cheese, etc. Or serve with ketchup or salsa.

Henry and Fannie Hertzler, Bloomsburg, PA

Fried Cabbage

4 slices bacon or ½ pound
   sausage, chopped
½ medium onion, chopped

½ medium head cabbage,
   coarsely chopped
1 tablespoon soy sauce

Brown bacon with onion. Drain excess fat. Add cabbage. Stir-fry over low heat until cabbage is tender. Add soy sauce. Serve over rice with additional soy sauce.

Lela Brenneman, Montezuma, GA

Zippy Vegetable Casserole

3 cups seeded and chopped
   fresh plum tomatoes
3 cups chopped zucchini
1 green pepper, chopped
½ teaspoon parsley flakes
½ teaspoon basil

¾ teaspoon garlic salt
1 cup shredded mozzarella
   cheese
2½ cups breadcrumbs
4 tablespoons butter,
   melted

Coat 9x13-inch baking dish with nonstick vegetable spray. Place tomatoes, zucchini, and green pepper in baking dish. Sprinkle with parsley flakes, basil, and garlic salt. Mix together cheese, breadcrumbs, and butter. Toss 1½ cups crumb mixture with veggies. Pour remaining crumbs over top of veggies. Bake at 350 degrees for about 45 minutes.

Note: Make ahead of time and store in refrigerator up to 24 hours before baking.

Esther Peachey, Fleminsburg, KY

MAIN DISHES

Mom's Galoushka
(German Stuffed Cabbage Rolls)

1 large head cabbage	¼ pound ground pork
1 to 2 tablespoons apple cider vinegar	½ teaspoon salt
1 cup cooked rice (white or brown)	¼ teaspoon pepper
1 pound ground beef	2 (15 ounce) cans tomato sauce

Place cabbage in kettle with just enough water to cover bottom of pan. Add apple cider vinegar to water. Cover kettle and steam until cabbage leaves turn a light color. Remove cabbage from kettle to cool. In large bowl, combine cooked rice, ground beef, ground pork, salt, and pepper. Mix well and form mixture into small balls, then roll in cooled cabbage leaves. Place in roasting pan and cover with tomato sauce. May add some water to bottom of pan for more moisture. Cover and bake at 350 degrees for 1½ hours. Good served with mashed potatoes.

Wanda Brunstetter

Honey BBQ Boneless Wings

BBQ Sauce:

3½ cups ketchup
⅔ cup vinegar
¾ cup molasses
¾ cup honey
2 teaspoons liquid smoke
2 teaspoons salt
2 teaspoons pepper

½ teaspoon paprika
1 teaspoon chili powder
¾ teaspoon onion powder
¾ teaspoon garlic powder
½ teaspoon cayenne pepper
(optional)

In saucepan, stir together all ingredients and simmer for 20 minutes, uncovered.

Breading:

6 cups flour
3 tablespoons salt
1½ tablespoons pepper
1 tablespoon paprika

2 teaspoons garlic powder
2 teaspoons cayenne pepper
(optional)

Mix together. Set aside.

Chicken:

5 pounds boneless chicken
   breasts
2 eggs

2 cups milk
Oil

Cut chicken into small pieces. In bowl, whisk together eggs and milk. Dip chicken pieces in egg mixture then in breading. Repeat this process so that chicken is double coated. Heat oil in skillet to 375 degrees. Deep-fry chicken for 5 to 7 minutes. Lay fried pieces on rack to dry a little. Put chicken in roaster in layers with BBQ sauce between layers and on top. Bake at 400 degrees for 15 minutes.

Susan Bontrager, Lagrange, IN

GRILLED CHICKEN

1 quart water
1 cup vinegar
½ cup corn oil
2 tablespoons
 Worcestershire sauce

3 tablespoons salt
½ tablespoon pepper
Chicken

Combine water, vinegar, oil, Worcestershire sauce, salt, and pepper. Add chicken and soak overnight. Grill chicken, using marinade to brush chicken as it cooks.

CLARA A. YODER, Sugar Grove, PA

SMOTHERED CHICKEN

3 tablespoons olive oil
1 teaspoon garlic powder
4 teaspoons chili powder
1 teaspoon salt
2 pounds chicken breast

⅔ cup mayonnaise
3 cups shredded Mexican
 cheese blend
Bacon bits

Combine olive oil, garlic powder, chili powder, and salt. Coat chicken and marinate for several hours (half a day is best). Heat grill and grill chicken until done on one side. Flip and slather on mayo then top with cheese and bacon bits. Grill until done through.

SUSAN YODER, Butler, OH

POPPY SEED CHICKEN

2 pounds chicken breasts
1 can cream of mushroom
 soup
1 cup sour cream

1½ cups crushed Ritz
 crackers
½ cup margarine, melted
1 teaspoon poppy seeds

Place chicken in baking dish. Mix soup and sour cream. Spread on chicken. Combine crackers and margarine. Stir in poppy seeds. Sprinkle on chicken. Bake at 350 degrees for 30 minutes.

MARIETTA BONTRAGER, Ligonier, IN

Chicken Burgers

4 pounds ground chicken
3 cups cracker crumbs
4 teaspoons chicken base
2 teaspoons Accent
4 teaspoons seasoned salt
1 teaspoon pepper
1 teaspoon salt
¼ cup brown sugar
1½ cups milk
2 cans cream of chicken soup
Flour
Oil for frying
Water

Mix chicken, crackers, chicken base, Accent, seasoned salt, pepper, salt, brown sugar, milk, and 1 can soup. Press in baking pan and let sit a few hours. Cut in squares and roll each in flour. Fry both sides to brown a little. Put in roaster in layers. Combine 1 can soup with 1 can water and pour over chicken. Bake at 350 degrees for 30 minutes.

Regina Bontrager, Lagrange, IN

Chicken-N-Stuffing Casserole

6 cups breadcrumbs, browned

¼ cup diced celery

1 tablespoon chopped onion

1 tablespoon parsley flakes

2 eggs

¼ cup butter

Salt and pepper to taste

Mix all ingredients and add hot water to moisten. Place in greased pan.

Topping:

¼ cup butter

4 tablespoons flour

1 cup chicken broth

1 can cream of chicken soup

1 soup can milk

1 whole chicken, cooked and cut up (or use canned chicken)

Salt and pepper to taste

Melt butter and thicken with flour to a paste. Add broth, soup, and milk. Cook until a thick gravy forms. Add chicken and season with salt and pepper. Pour over breadcrumb mixture. Bake at 350 degrees for 40 to 45 minutes until bubbly.

Betty H. Byler, Smicksburg, PA

Chipotle Chicken Haystack

Chicken:

2 tablespoons lemon juice
1½ teaspoons seasoned salt
1½ teaspoons cumin
1 teaspoon garlic salt
½ teaspoon chili powder
½ teaspoon paprika
1½ pounds chicken breast, diced
Coconut oil for frying

Combine lemon juice, seasoned salt, cumin, garlic salt, chili powder, and paprika. Marinate chicken in seasonings for at least 4 hours. Fry in coconut oil until done.

Rice:

2 cups rice
2 tablespoons coconut oil
½ teaspoon pepper
1 teaspoon salt
4 teaspoons chicken soup base
1 teaspoon cumin
1 teaspoon oregano
1 teaspoon garlic powder
1 to 2 tablespoons cilantro flakes
5 cups water

Fry rice in coconut oil for a couple of minutes, stirring often. Add remaining ingredients and simmer, covered, for 1 hour and 15 minutes until rice is tender.

Beans:

1 (15 ounce) can black beans, undrained
½ teaspoon cumin
1 teaspoon chili powder
¾ teaspoon lemon pepper
½ teaspoon salt
1 tablespoon cilantro flakes

Simmer all in saucepan for 10 minutes; drain.

Toppings:

1 (15 ounce) can whole kernel corn, warmed and drained
Salsa
Sour cream
Guacamole
Shredded cheese
Chopped lettuce

Make your own chipotle stack with toppings of your choice. You can also wrap your stack in a large tortilla.

Cheyann Miller, Kalona, IA

Cordon Bleu Casserole

4 cups cubed cooked turkey
4 cups cubed cooked ham
1 cup shredded cheese
1 cup diced onion
¼ cup butter

⅓ cup flour
2 cups cream
1 teaspoon dill weed
⅛ teaspoon dry mustard
⅛ teaspoon nutmeg

Combine turkey, ham, and cheese. Set aside. Sauté onion in butter until tender; add flour to form a paste. Gradually add cream, stirring constantly. Bring to a boil. Boil 1 minute or until thick. Add dill weed, mustard, and nutmeg; mix well. Pour over meat and mix. Pour into greased 9x13-inch casserole dish.

Topping:

1 cup dry breadcrumbs
2 tablespoons butter
¼ teaspoon dill weed

¼ cup shredded cheese
¼ cup walnuts, chopped

Toss together breadcrumbs, butter, and dill weed. Stir in cheese and walnuts. Sprinkle over casserole. Bake at 350 degrees, uncovered, for 30 minutes or until heated.

Mabel Yoder, Mount Vernon, OH

Spicy Chicken Casserole

1½ cups chopped onion
2 cups chopped bell pepper
½ cup butter
1 (12 ounce) package spiral
  noodles, cooked in
  chicken broth
1 pound Velveeta cheese
1 can cream of mushroom
  soup

1 can mild Ro-Tel tomatoes
½ teaspoon garlic salt
1 teaspoon chicken
  seasoning
½ teaspoon salt
¼ teaspoon pepper
½ teaspoon seasoned salt
4 cups chopped cooked
  chicken

Sauté onion and peppers in butter. Add to cooked noodles. Mix in cheese, mushroom soup, tomatoes, garlic salt, chicken seasoning, salt, pepper, and seasoned salt. Stir until cheese melts. Add chicken. Additional broth can be added to moisten as desired. Bake at 350 degrees for 30 minutes or until hot and bubbly.

Lela Brenneman, Montezuma, GA

Ginger Stir-Fry

2 tablespoons cornstarch
1 cup beef or chicken broth
3 tablespoons soy sauce
1 tablespoon sugar
1½ teaspoons ginger
½ teaspoon garlic powder

½ teaspoon red pepper flakes
Stir-fried vegetables
Cooked meat
Cooked rice

Mix together cornstarch and broth. In saucepan, combine broth with soy sauce, sugar, ginger, garlic powder, and red pepper flakes. Cook until thick. Pour over crisp-tender stir-fried vegetables of your choice (e.g., cabbage, celery, onions, carrots, bell peppers, summer squash, asparagus, green beans, snow peas). Add meat of your choice. Serve over rice.

LELA BRENNEMAN, Montezuma, GA

Cowboy Hash

2 pounds ground beef
1 cup pork and beans
1 cup ketchup
4 cups mixed vegetables

4 tablespoons yellow
mustard
¼ cup brown sugar

Brown beef. Stir in beans, ketchup, vegetables, mustard, and brown sugar. Heat thoroughly. Good served with corn bread.

MARY PETERSHEIM, Apple Creek, OH

Overnight Casserole

2 cups meat (chicken, ham,
or beef)
2 cups milk
2 cups uncooked macaroni

2 cans cream of chicken
soup
½ pound diced Velveeta
cheese
1 cup peas

Mix and let sit overnight in refrigerator. Bake in 9x13-inch pan at 350 degrees for 1 hour.

AMANDA ROSE ESH, Parkesburg, PA

Tater Tot Hot Dish

1½ pounds ground beef,
browned
1 cup chopped onion
3 cups chopped celery

1 can cream of chicken soup
1 can cream of mushroom
soup
1 pound tater tots

Combine beef, onion, celery, chicken soup, and mushroom soup. Pour into baking dish. Top with tater tots. Bake at 350 degrees for 1 hour.

IRENE A. SCHWARTZ, Monroe, IN

Glazed Meat Loaf

1½ pounds ground beef
¾ cup quick oats
½ cup milk
¼ cup finely chopped onion
1 egg, beaten
1 teaspoon Worcestershire
   sauce

1 teaspoon salt
⅛ teaspoon pepper
¼ cup apple cider vinegar
½ cup brown sugar
½ teaspoon dry mustard
1 teaspoon Worcestershire
   sauce

Combine beef, oats, milk, onion, egg, 1 teaspoon Worcestershire sauce, salt, and pepper. Mix well with hands. Press into 9x5x3-inch pan. Blend vinegar, brown sugar, mustard, and 1 teaspoon Worcestershire sauce. Spoon sauce on top of meat and bake at 350 degrees for 45 to 50 minutes.

JILL (RENSBERGER) BANSBACK, Granger, IN

Meat Loaf Pie

1 (5 ounce) can evaporated
   milk
½ cup dry breadcrumbs
½ teaspoon garlic salt
1 pound lean ground beef
⅓ cup ketchup

1 cup shredded cheddar
   cheese
½ teaspoon oregano
1 tablespoon grated
   Parmesan cheese

In bowl, combine milk, breadcrumbs, and garlic salt. Add beef and mix well. Press meat mixture into bottom and 1 inch up sides of greased 9-inch pie pan. Bake, uncovered, at 350 degrees for 20 minutes. Drain off any grease. Spread with ketchup and sprinkle with cheddar cheese, oregano, and Parmesan cheese. Bake 3 to 5 minutes. It is done when meat is no longer pink and cheese is melted. Yield: 4 servings.

LENA YODER, McClure, PA

Tangy Meatballs

3 pounds ground beef or
  venison
2 cups oats
1 cup milk
2 eggs

1½ cups chopped onion
2 teaspoons salt
1 teaspoon pepper
1 teaspoon garlic powder

Combine all ingredients and roll into 1½-inch balls. Place in two 9x13-inch baking pans. Bake uncovered at 375 degrees for 30 minutes. Remove from oven, drain fat, and combine in 1 pan. Pour on sauce and bake uncovered for 20 minutes.

Sauce:

2 cups ketchup
1½ cups brown sugar
½ cup chopped onion

2½ teaspoons liquid smoke
1 teaspoon garlic powder

In bowl, mix all ingredients together.

Daniel and Laura Schwartz, Carlisle, KY

Poor Man's Steak

2 pounds ground beef
2 cups cracker crumbs
2 cups milk
2 teaspoons salt
½ teaspoon pepper

1 cup chopped onion
Flour
1 cup water
1 (10¾ ounces) can cream of
    mushroom soup

Mix beef, cracker crumbs, milk, salt, pepper, and onion. Press into patties. Roll in flour and fry on both sides until browned. Put in roaster. Mix soup and water. Pour over top. Bake at 350 degrees for 30 minutes. Yield: 6 servings.

Martha Schmucker, Sturgis, MI

Pizza Burgers

Sliced bread
Hamburger patties
Chopped onion

Pizza sauce
Mozzarella cheese, sliced or shredded

Line cookie sheet with slices of bread. Fry hamburger patties. Cook onion in drippings. Spoon pizza sauce on each slice of bread. Add 1 hamburger and some onion to each slice. Top with cheese. Bake at 350 degrees for about 15 minutes.

Mrs. Abe L. Yoder, Apple Creek, OH

Shrimp-in-Love Pasta

¼ pound linguine
1 cup raw medium shrimp, deveined and peeled

2 tomatoes, chopped
½ cup cream cheese
1½ cups torn fresh spinach

Cook linguine as directed on package. Meanwhile, heat large skillet over medium-high heat. Add shrimp, tomatoes, and cream cheese; cook and stir 3 to 4 minutes, or until shrimp are done and mixture is well blended. Drain linguine and place in large bowl. Add spinach and mix lightly. Stir in shrimp mixture.

Rosanna Petersheim, Junction City, OH

Potato Stack Casserole

8 medium potatoes, cooked
and shredded
1 cup sour cream
1 cup milk
1 package ranch dressing
mix

2 pounds ground beef
1 package taco seasoning
3 cups cheese sauce
Nacho-flavored chips

Place potatoes in roaster. Mix sour cream, milk, and ranch dressing mix. Pour on top of potatoes. Brown beef. Add taco seasoning. Put on top of cream layer. Pour cheese sauce over meat layer. Bake at 350 degrees for 30 minutes. Before serving, top with crushed chips.

Ruby Bontrager, Lagrange, IN

Garbage Fries

1½ to 2 pounds cooked
french fries
1 batch sloppy joe meat
1 medium green pepper,
julienned

Hot peppers (optional)
1 batch cheese sauce (see
page 192)
Bacon, fried and crumbled

Prepare each plate starting with a pile of french fries. Top with sloppy joe meat, green peppers, hot peppers, cheese sauce, and bacon. Delicious and filling.

Mrs. Reuben (Martha) Byler, Atlantic, PA

Lasagna

2 pounds ground beef
2½ cups pizza sauce
2¼ cups tomato juice
¼ teaspoon salt
1 teaspoon pepper
¼ teaspoon oregano

8 ounces lasagna noodles
2 tablespoons salad oil
1 pound Velveeta cheese
Parmesan or mozzarella
  cheese

Fry beef until brown. Add pizza sauce, tomato juice, salt, pepper, and oregano. Cover and simmer for 20 minutes. Don't thin sauce. In pot of boiling salted water, cook noodles with oil until tender. In casserole pan, layer meat sauce, noodles, and cheese until everything is used. Bake at 325 degrees for 20 to 30 minutes, covered, until bubbly hot and cheese melts.

LOVINA M. SCHWARTZ, Geneva, IN

Pizza Pockets

2 tablespoons yeast
1½ cups warm water
6 tablespoons brown sugar
4½ cups bread flour
Pizza sauce

Cooked meat (ground beef, sausage, smokies, and/or pepperoni)
Mozzarella cheese
2 teaspoons baking soda
Oregano
Melted butter

Dissolve yeast in water. Add brown sugar. Vigorously stir in flour. Let rise. Roll out dough and cut in wide strips. Spread pizza sauce on center of each strip. Top with meat and cheese. Fold dough over filling and pinch edges. Cut away any extra dough on ends. Dissolve baking soda in bowl of water. Dip pockets in soda water. Place on greased baking sheet and sprinkle with oregano. Bake at 400 degrees for 25 to 30 minutes until light brown. Brush with melted butter.

Mary Schwartz, Berne, IN
Mrs. Benjamin Wickey, Monroe, IN

Dad's Savory Stew

1 pound stew meat,
  browned
1 cup chopped carrots
1 cup chopped turnips
1 cup chopped celery
1 cup chopped onion
2 cups chopped potatoes
½ teaspoon thyme
½ teaspoon sage
½ teaspoon poultry
  seasoning

Combine all ingredients in large kettle or Dutch oven. Cook 30 minutes or until meat and vegetables are tender. Thicken to your liking with flour and milk. Serve as is or with dumplings, bread, or biscuits.

WANDA BRUNSTETTER

Hearty Hamburger Soup

1 pound ground beef
1 cup chopped onion
1 cup chopped green pepper
1 cup sliced carrots
1 cup diced potatoes
3 cups tomato juice
1½ teaspoons salt
½ teaspoon pepper
1 teaspoon chili powder
1 teaspoon Italian
  seasoning

In large pot, fry beef; add onion and peppers. Fry a couple more minutes. Add carrots, potatoes, tomato juice, salt, pepper, chili powder, and Italian seasoning. Cover and cook until vegetables are tender.

MOSES RIEHL, Coatsville, PA

Zucchini Sausage Casserole

1 pound sausage, browned
   and drained
1 (14 ounce) can cream of
   mushroom soup
14 saltine crackers, crushed
4 to 6 cups diced zucchini

2 eggs, beaten
¼ cup diced onion
Salt and pepper to taste
1 cup shredded cheese

Mix sausage, soup, crackers, zucchini, eggs, onion, and salt and pepper. Pour in greased 9x13-inch casserole dish. Bake uncovered at 325 degrees for 1 hour, then top with cheese and return to oven until melted.

MABEL YODER, Mount Vernon, OH

Sausage Potato Soup

6 medium potatoes, cubed
2 cups frozen corn
2½ cups chicken broth
½ cup chopped celery
¼ cup sliced carrots
½ teaspoon garlic powder

½ teaspoon onion powder
½ teaspoon salt
¼ teaspoon pepper
1½ cups milk
1 cup Velveeta cheese
1 pound sausage, fried

Combine potatoes, corn, broth, celery, carrots, garlic powder, onion powder, salt, and pepper. Bring to a boil and reduce heat. Cover and simmer for 15 minutes until vegetables are tender. Add milk, cheese, and sausage. Heat until cheese is melted.

MOSES RIEHL, Coatsville, PA

DESSERTS

Bars and Cookies

FUDGE NUT BARS

1 cup butter	2 cups flour
2 cups brown sugar	1 teaspoon baking soda
2 eggs, beaten	1 teaspoon salt
2 teaspoons vanilla	3 cups quick oats

Cream butter and brown sugar. Add eggs and vanilla. Add flour, baking soda, and salt. Mix well. Add oats. Mix well. Spread two-thirds of dough in jelly roll pan. Cover with chocolate mixture. Top with remaining dough. Bake at 350 degrees for 25 to 30 minutes.

CHOCOLATE MIXTURE:

2 tablespoons butter	½ teaspoon salt
1 cup chocolate chips	1 cup nuts
1 can sweetened condensed milk	2 teaspoons vanilla

In saucepan, combine butter, chocolate chips, milk, and salt. Stir until melted. Add nuts and vanilla.

EMMA ZOOK, Navarre, OH

MONSTER COOKIE BARS

½ cup margarine or butter, melted	1 teaspoon corn syrup
1½ cups creamy peanut butter	4 cups oats
1 cup sugar	2 teaspoons baking soda
1¼ cups brown sugar	1 cup M&M's
3 eggs	¾ cup chocolate chips

Mix all ingredients in order given. Spread in jelly roll pan (9x13-inch pan will also work). Bake at 350 degrees for 15 to 20 minutes. Do not overbake. You could also form into cookies instead of bars.

DAVID L. BYLER, New Wilmington, PA

HONEY BUN BARS

3 eggs, separated
1½ cups sugar
2¼ cups sifted flour
3 teaspoons baking powder
1 teaspoon salt
⅓ cup oil

1 cup water
1 teaspoon vanilla
3½ tablespoons sucanat or
  brown sugar
2½ teaspoons cinnamon

Beat egg whites until frothy. Gradually add ½ cup sugar. Beat until stiff and glossy. In another bowl sift remaining sugar, flour, baking powder, and salt. Add oil, water, egg yolks, and vanilla. Beat until smooth. Fold in egg whites. Pour half of batter into 10x15-inch pan. Combine sucanat and cinnamon and sprinkle over top. Add remaining batter. Bake at 350 degrees for 40 minutes.

FROSTING:

¼ cup butter
⅓ scant cup sucanat
⅛ cup water

3 ounces cream cheese
½ teaspoon vanilla

In saucepan, brown butter for 5 minutes. Add sucanat and water. Cook 5 minutes. Remove from heat and add cream cheese and vanilla, beating until smooth. Spread on top of buns.

MARTHA MILLER, Gallipolis, OH

Coffee Shop Brownies

1½ cups sugar	9 tablespoons cocoa powder
¾ cup butter, melted	¾ cup flour
¾ teaspoon vanilla	½ teaspoon baking powder
3 eggs	

Mix all together and spread into 9x13-inch pan.

Filling:

3 (8 ounce) packages cream cheese	½ cup strong coffee
3 eggs, beaten	1½ cups sugar
	Chopped pecans (optional)

Blend cream cheese with eggs, coffee, and sugar until smooth. Spread over brownie batter. Sprinkle with pecans if desired. Bake at 350 degrees for 45 minutes until set. Cool.

Topping:

¾ cup chocolate chips	Caramel sauce (optional)
2 tablespoons milk	

Melt chocolate chips. Add milk and mix until smooth. Drizzle over top of brownies. You can also drizzle caramel sauce on top if desired.

ANNA MILLER, Loudonville, OH

Hawaiian Cheesecake Bars

2 cups flour
1 cup sugar
1 cup butter, softened
2 (8 ounce) packages cream
  cheese
4 tablespoons sugar
4 tablespoons milk

2 eggs
2 teaspoons vanilla
2 (8 ounce) cans crushed
  pineapple
2 cups shredded coconut
2 tablespoons melted butter

Combine flour, 1 cup sugar, and softened butter. Pat in 9x13-inch pan and bake at 350 degrees for 15 minutes until browned around edges. Blend cream cheese, 4 tablespoons sugar, milk, and eggs. Fold in vanilla and pineapple. Spread over crust. Mix coconut and melted butter and sprinkle over pineapple. Bake 15 to 20 minutes or until coconut is slightly toasted.

BECKY FISHER, Lancaster, PA

Chocolate Chip Cheesecake Bars

¾ cup shortening
¾ cup sugar
⅓ cup brown sugar
1 egg
1½ teaspoons vanilla
1½ cups flour
1 teaspoon salt
¾ teaspoon baking soda

1½ cups chocolate chips
¾ cup chopped walnuts
2 (8 ounce) packages cream
  cheese
¾ cup sugar
2 eggs
1 teaspoon vanilla

Cream shortening, ¾ cup sugar, and brown sugar. Add 1 egg and 1½ teaspoons vanilla. Combine flour, salt, and baking soda. Add to creamed mixture and mix well. Fold in chocolate chips and nuts. Set aside one-third of dough for topping. Press remaining dough into greased 9x13-inch pan. Bake at 350 degrees for 8 minutes. Meanwhile, beat cream cheese and ¾ cup sugar until smooth. Add 2 eggs and 1 teaspoon vanilla. Mix well. Spoon over crust. Drop teaspoonfuls of dough over filling. Bake at 350 degrees for 35 to 40 minutes until golden brown.

ABNER AND AMANDA MILLER, Wisconsin Rapids, WI

Fudge Brownies

1 (12 ounce) package
    semisweet chocolate
    chips
1 cup margarine or butter
4 eggs

2 cups sugar
1 teaspoon vanilla
2 cups flour
1 cup chopped pecans

Combine chocolate chips and margarine in saucepan over low heat. Stir until melted and well blended. Set aside to cool slightly. In bowl, beat eggs with whisk until lightly beaten. Beat in sugar, vanilla, and melted chocolate. Stir in flour. Add nuts. Pour in greased 9x13-inch pan. Bake at 325 degrees for 35 to 40 minutes or until pulled away from edges of pan and set in center.

Mrs. Enos (Maria) Wickey, Monroe, IN

No-Bake Bars

1 cup peanut butter
½ cup honey
¼ cup cocoa powder

3 cups oats
¼ cup chopped nuts
    (optional)

In medium saucepan, heat peanut butter, honey, and cocoa. Add oats and nuts, stirring well. Press in waxed paper–lined 8x8-inch pan. Chill a few minutes. Cut into squares.

Susie L. Schwartz, Geneva, IN

Pumpkin Bars

4 eggs
1 cup salad oil
2 cups sugar
1 cup canned pumpkin
½ teaspoon salt

2 teaspoons cinnamon
1 teaspoon baking soda
2 teaspoons baking powder
2 cups flour

Combine all ingredients and pour into greased large cookie sheet. Bake at 350 degrees for 20 to 25 minutes.

Martha Miller, Gallipolis, OH

Marshmallow Brownies

1½ cups flour
½ teaspoon salt
½ teaspoon baking powder
4 tablespoons cocoa powder
1 cup shortening
1½ cups sugar

4 eggs
1½ teaspoons vanilla
¾ cup chopped nuts
2 cups mini marshmallows
Chocolate frosting

Sift together flour, salt, baking powder, and cocoa. Cream together shortening and sugar. Add eggs, vanilla, and nuts. Add dry ingredients. Spread on large cookie sheet. Bake at 350 degrees for 25 to 30 minutes. When baked, add marshmallows on top. Put back in oven until you can spread marshmallows. Frost with chocolate frosting when cool.

Mrs. Yost (Lizzie) Borntrager, Bethany, MO

Peanut Butter Bars

1 cup peanut butter
6 tablespoons butter,
 softened
1¼ cups sugar
3 eggs

1 teaspoon vanilla
1 cup flour
¼ teaspoon salt
2 cups chocolate chips,
 divided

Beat together peanut butter, butter, and sugar. Add eggs and vanilla. Mix in flour and salt. Fold in 1 cup chocolate chips. Spread in ungreased 9x13-inch pan. Bake at 350 degrees for 25 to 30 minutes until edges begin to brown. Immediately sprinkle remaining 1 cup chocolate chips on top. When softened, spread over top. Cool before cutting and serving.

Mrs. Velma Schrock, Goshen, IN

Toffee Bars

1 cup plus 2 tablespoons
  butter (no substitutes)
2½ cups flour
½ cup sugar
1 cup butter (no substitutes)

1 cup brown sugar
1 can evaporated milk
4 tablespoons corn syrup
12 ounces milk chocolate
  chips

Mix 1 cup plus 2 tablespoons butter, flour, and sugar until crumbly. Press into jelly roll pan. Bake at 350 degrees for 20 minutes. In saucepan, bring 1 cup butter, brown sugar, evaporated milk, and corn syrup to a boil for 5 minutes. Pour over crust and cool. Melt chocolate chips and pour over top. Cool.

AMANDA BYLER, Curwensville, PA

Yum Yum Bars

4 cups flour
1 cup butter or margarine
1 cup brown sugar
6 eggs
4 cups brown sugar

1 teaspoon salt
2 cups shredded coconut
4 tablespoons flour
½ teaspoon baking powder
2 teaspoons vanilla

Mix together 4 cups flour, butter, and 1 cup brown sugar and press into bottom of large cookie sheet. Blend eggs, 4 cups brown sugar, salt, coconut, 4 tablespoons flour, baking powder, and vanilla. Spread over first layer. Bake at 350 degrees for 20 minutes or until nice and brown.

KATIE R. HOSTETLER, Smicksburg, PA

No-Bake Cookies

½ cup sugar
½ cup honey
3 tablespoons cocoa powder
¼ cup butter
½ cup milk
3 cups oats
¾ cup peanut butter

1 teaspoon vanilla
¾ cup chopped nuts
¼ cup unsweetened shredded coconut
1 scoop protein powder (optional)

In saucepan, bring to a boil sugar, honey, cocoa, butter, and milk. Cook for 1 minute. Remove from heat and add oats, peanut butter, vanilla, nuts, coconut, and protein powder. Drop by teaspoonfuls onto waxed paper and chill.

MARYANN STAUFFER, Homer City, PA

Children's Delight Cookies

1 cup sugar
1 cup brown sugar
1 cup shortening
2 eggs
1 teaspoon vanilla
2 cups flour

½ teaspoon salt
1 teaspoon baking soda
1 teaspoon baking powder
2 cups oats
½ cup chopped nuts
1 cup chocolate chips

Cream together sugar, brown sugar, and shortening. Add eggs, flour, salt, baking soda, and baking powder. Mix well. Add oats, nuts, vanilla, and chocolate chips. Drop by teaspoonfuls on cookie sheet. Flatten slightly. Bake at 350 degrees for 10 to 12 minutes. Can be frosted with your favorite frosting.

SUSANNA MILLER, Decatur, IN

COOKIE SHEET WHOOPIES

1½ cups margarine
3½ cups sugar
4 eggs
2 teaspoons vanilla
4 cups flour

1½ cups cocoa powder
2½ teaspoons baking soda
1 teaspoon salt
2⅔ cups water

Cream margarine and sugar. Add eggs and vanilla. Add flour, cocoa powder, baking soda, and salt. Gradually add water. Mix well and divide into 2 greased cookie sheets. Bake at 375 degrees for 20 to 25 minutes until done. Cool. Top one cake with your choice of whoopie pie filling, then top with other cake. Cut into squares.

EMMA ZOOK, Navarre, OH

Chocolate Crinkles

½ cup butter
2 cups sugar
4 eggs
2 teaspoons vanilla
4 cups flour

½ cup cocoa powder
2 teaspoons baking powder
½ teaspoon salt
Powdered sugar

Mix butter, sugar, eggs, and vanilla. Add flour, cocoa, baking powder, and salt. Mix well and chill for several hours. Form balls and roll balls in powdered sugar. Bake at 350 degrees for 10 to 12 minutes or until done. You can put cream filling in between 2 cookies for whoopie pies.

MARTHA BEECHY, Butler, OH

Chocolate Chip Cookies

2 cups butter
½ cup sugar
¾ cup brown sugar
4 eggs
2 teaspoons vanilla
4½ cups flour

2 teaspoons baking soda
2 (3 ounce) boxes instant
vanilla pudding mix
2 (12 ounce) packages
chocolate chips

Cream together butter, sugar, and brown sugar until smooth. Beat in eggs one at a time, then stir in vanilla. Combine flour, baking soda, and pudding mix. Mix into first mixture. Stir in chocolate chips. Drop by large spoonfuls on ungreased pans. Bake at 350 degrees for 10 to 12 minutes.

SARAH BEILER, Doylesburg, PA

Clara's Chocolate Chip Cookies

3½ cups brown sugar
1 cup shortening
1 cup margarine
¼ cup molasses
3 eggs

3 teaspoons vanilla
1 teaspoon salt
3 teaspoons baking soda
6 cups flour
2 cups chocolate chips

Cream together brown sugar, shortening, margarine, and molasses. Add eggs and vanilla. Mix in salt, baking soda, and flour. Add chocolate chips. Bake at 375 degrees for 10 to 12 minutes.

CLARA A. YODER, Sugar Grove, PA

Honey Sugar Cookies

2 cups sugar
2 cups brown sugar
2 cups butter, softened
1 cup shortening
1 cup honey
4 eggs

6 teaspoons baking soda
9 cups flour
1 teaspoon salt
1 cup sugar
2 teaspoons cinnamon

Cream 2 cups sugar, brown sugar, butter, and shortening. Add honey; mix well. Add eggs; beat. Work in baking soda, flour, and salt. In small bowl, combine 1 cup sugar and cinnamon. Shape dough into balls. Roll each ball in cinnamon-sugar mixture. Bake at 350 degrees for 8 to 10 minutes until golden brown.

"These are very chewy and delicious!"

Mary Wagler, Montgomery, IN

Ginger Cookies

2 cups dark molasses
1 egg
1 cup lard
4 teaspoons baking soda
1 cup boiling water
2 tablespoons vinegar

¾ teaspoon salt
½ teaspoon cinnamon
2 tablespoons ginger
6 to 8 cups flour
1 cup sugar

Mix molasses, egg, and lard. Dissolve baking soda in boiling water, then add to molasses mixture. Add vinegar, salt, cinnamon, ginger, and flour. Mix well into dough. Cover and refrigerate 1 hour. Make dough into balls and dip in sugar. Flatten a bit on cookie sheets. Bake at 350 degrees for 10 minutes.

Martha Yoder, Port Royal, PA

Pecan Sandies

½ cup butter or margarine, softened
¼ cup sugar
1 teaspoon vanilla

1 cup cake flour
½ cup finely chopped pecans

In mixing bowl, cream butter and sugar until well blended. Stir in vanilla. Add flour. Mix on low until well blended. Stir in pecans; mix well. Chill for 30 minutes. Roll into 1-inch balls. Place on greased baking sheet. Bake at 350 degrees for 15 to 18 minutes or until bottom edges are golden brown. Cool on wire rack. Yield: about 1½ dozen.

MARTHA YODER, Port Royal, PA

Pumpkin Chip Cookies

2 cups canned pumpkin
2 cups sugar
1 cup vegetable oil or
    shortening
2 eggs, beaten
2 tablespoons milk
2 teaspoons vanilla

4 cups flour
2 teaspoons baking soda
4 teaspoons baking powder
1 teaspoon salt
2 teaspoons cinnamon
1 package chocolate chips
1 cup chopped nuts

Mix pumpkin, sugar, oil, eggs, milk, and vanilla. In another bowl, sift together flour, baking soda, baking powder, salt, and cinnamon. Gradually add to first mixture. Add chocolate chips and nuts. Drop by spoonfuls on cookie sheets. Bake at 375 degrees for 10 minutes.

"Very moist and good!"

Mrs. Eli A. Kurtz, Dayton, PA

Pineapple Cookies

2 cups flour
1 teaspoon baking powder
1 teaspoon baking soda
1 teaspoon salt
½ cup shortening, softened
1 egg

1 teaspoon vanilla
½ cup crushed pineapple, drained
¼ tablespoon nutmeg
1 heaping tablespoon sugar

Mix flour, baking powder, baking soda, and salt. In another bowl, combine shortening, egg, and vanilla; mix until creamy. Add to first mixture and mix well. Add pineapple. Drop by teaspoonfuls on cookie sheets. Combine nutmeg and sugar and sprinkle on cookies. Bake at 325 degrees for 8 to 10 minutes for a soft cookie.

ESTHER M. SCHWARTZ, Geneva, IN

Snickerdoodles

2¾ cups flour
3 teaspoons baking powder
½ teaspoon salt
1½ cups sugar
1 cup butter or shortening, softened

2 eggs, beaten
4 teaspoons cinnamon
4 tablespoons sugar

Sift together flour, baking powder, and salt. In separate bowl, cream 1½ cups sugar and butter until fluffy. Add eggs and mix. Gradually add sifted mixture. Mix well. Chill. Roll teaspoonfuls of dough into small balls. Combine cinnamon and 4 tablespoons sugar and roll dough in mixture. Place 2 inches apart on ungreased baking sheet. Bake at 400 degrees for 10 minutes.

VERNIE SCHWARTZ, Stanwood, MI

Soft Sugar Cookies with Frosting

8 cups flour
4 teaspoons baking powder
2 teaspoons salt
3 sticks butter or
    margarine, softened

3 cups sugar
4 eggs
3 teaspoons vanilla

Combine flour, baking powder, and salt. In large bowl, beat butter with sugar. Add eggs and vanilla; beat well. Stir in dry ingredients one-third at a time. Drop by tablespoonfuls onto greased cookie sheet. Bake at 350 degrees for 8 to 10 minutes.

Frosting:

¼ cup butter (no substitutes)
3 tablespoons boiling water

½ teaspoon vanilla
2 cups powdered sugar

Blend butter, water, and vanilla. Slowly beat in powdered sugar. Frost cooled cookies.

Mrs. Enos (Maria) Wickey, Monroe, IN

Cakes

APPLE CAKE

2 eggs
4 cups sliced apples
½ cup oil
1 teaspoon vanilla
1 cup chopped nuts

2 cups flour
2 cups sugar
½ teaspoon salt
2 teaspoons baking soda
½ teaspoon cinnamon

In mixing bowl, break eggs over apples and stir well to coat. Add oil, vanilla, nuts, flour, sugar, salt, baking soda, and cinnamon. Stir well. Pour into greased and floured 9x13-inch pan. Bake at 350 degrees for 1 hour. Serve with sauce while cake is still warm.

SAUCE:

1 tablespoon flour
½ cup brown sugar

1½ teaspoons vanilla
½ cup milk

In saucepan, combine ingredients and cook just until hot and thickened.

MRS. ORIE DETWEILER, Inola, OK

BROWN BETTY

1 cup quick oats
1 cup flour
¾ cup brown sugar
Pinch salt

1 teaspoon baking soda
½ cup butter
2 cups sliced or shredded apples

Mix oats, flour, brown sugar, salt, and baking soda. Blend in butter. Spread half of batter in 4x9-inch pan. Top with apples. Crumble remaining batter on top. Bake at 350 degrees for 30 minutes.

VERNA STUTZMAN, Navarre, OH

Delicious Apple Cake

1 cup sugar
½ cup brown sugar
1 cup shortening
2 eggs, beaten
1 cup sour milk
2 cups diced apples

1 teaspoon salt
2¾ cups flour
1 teaspoon baking soda
½ cup brown sugar
½ cup nuts
1 teaspoon cinnamon

In mixing bowl, cream sugar, ½ cup brown sugar, and shortening. Add eggs and milk. Mix in apples. In small bowl, mix together salt, flour, and baking soda. Mix into first mixture. Spread into greased 9x13-inch pan. In small bowl, combine ½ cup brown sugar, nuts, and cinnamon. Sprinkle over cake batter. Bake at 350 degrees for 45 to 50 minutes, until toothpick comes out clean.

Dorcas Marie Yoder, Meyersdale, PA

Blueberry Kuchen

1½ cups flour
¾ cup sugar
2 teaspoons baking powder
½ teaspoon nutmeg
¼ teaspoon salt

⅔ cup milk
¼ cup butter, melted
1 egg, beaten
1 teaspoon vanilla
1¼ cups blueberries

In mixing bowl, mix flour, sugar, baking powder, nutmeg, and salt. Add milk, butter, egg, and vanilla. Beat well. Pour in greased 9x13-inch pan. Sprinkle with blueberries. Add topping.

Topping:

¾ cup sugar
½ cup flour

¼ cup butter, melted

Mix together and sprinkle over blueberries. Bake at 350 degrees for 40 minutes or until done.

Lorene Byler, Irvington, KY

One Egg Banana Cake

2 cups flour
1¼ cups sugar
1 teaspoon baking soda
1 teaspoon baking powder
1 teaspoon salt

½ cup shortening
½ cup sour milk
1 cup mashed bananas
1 egg
1 teaspoon vanilla

Mix all and bake at 350 degrees for 30 minutes until done.

Betty H. Byler, Smicksburg, PA

Hawaiian Carrot Cake

2 cups spelt flour
2 teaspoons baking powder
1½ teaspoons baking soda
1 teaspoon salt
2 teaspoons cinnamon
½ cup nuts

¾ cup sucanat
¾ cup oil
4 eggs
2 cups finely grated carrots
2 cups coconut
1 cup crushed pineapple

Mix dry ingredients. Add oil and eggs and mix thoroughly. Stir in carrots, coconut, and pineapple. Mix well. Pour in greased 9x13-inch pan. Bake at 350 degrees for 35 to 40 minutes. Set pan on rack to cool.

Cream Cheese Frosting:

1 (8 ounce) package cream cheese
6 tablespoons butter, softened

4 tablespoons honey
1 teaspoon cinnamon

Beat cream cheese until smooth. Add butter and beat until fluffy. Add honey and cinnamon, mixing in well. Spread on cooled cake.

Tip: To make a layer cake, divide batter between two 9-inch layer pans. Cool baked layers before turning out on racks. Double frosting recipe and use between layers. May need another batch or two of frosting to finish top and sides.

Rebecca J. Hershberger, Dalton, OH

Herman Carrot Cake

2 cups flour
2 cups sugar
1 teaspoon salt
1 teaspoon baking powder
1 teaspoon baking soda
1 teaspoon cinnamon
2 cups shredded carrots

1 cup vegetable oil
1 cup Herman starter (see page 31)
4 eggs, beaten
Cream cheese frosting
½ cup chopped nuts

Sift together flour, sugar, salt, baking powder, baking soda, and cinnamon. Add carrots, oil, Herman, and eggs. Mix until moistened then beat. Pour into greased pan. Bake at 325 degrees for 55 minutes. Cool. After completely cooled, spread with cream cheese frosting. Sprinkle with nuts.

Martha Beechy, Butler, OH

THE 10-DAY HERMAN CAKE

1 cup sugar

2 eggs

2 cups Herman starter
(see page 31)

2 cups flour

¾ cup milk

½ teaspoon baking soda

½ teaspoon baking powder

2 teaspoons salt

1½ teaspoons cinnamon

⅔ cup oil

1 cup chopped nuts

1 cup raisins

1 tablespoon flour

1 cup brown sugar

1 tablespoon cinnamon

¼ cup butter, softened

Before you bake, be sure to reserve 1 cup Herman to start again.

Mix sugar, eggs, Herman, 2 cups flour, milk, baking soda, baking powder, salt, 1½ teaspoons cinnamon, and oil at medium speed; add nuts and raisins. Put in greased pan. Combine 1 tablespoon flour, brown sugar, 1 tablespoon cinnamon, and butter and sprinkle on cake batter. Bake at 350 degrees for 30 to 40 minutes.

MARTHA BEECHY, Butler, OH

CHOCOLATE FUDGE CAKE

½ cup butter, softened
1½ cups sugar
2 large eggs
1 teaspoon vanilla
½ cup plus 1 tablespoon hot
   water

⅔ cup cocoa powder
1¾ cups flour
1 teaspoon baking soda
1 teaspoon baking powder
½ teaspoon salt
1 cup sour milk

Combine butter and sugar until fluffy. Add eggs one at a time, beating well after each addition. Mix in vanilla. In small bowl, stir hot water into cocoa powder to make a paste. Gradually add cocoa to first mixture. Set aside. In another bowl, combine flour, baking soda, baking powder, and salt. Add flour mixture to creamed mixture alternately with sour milk. Pour batter into 2 greased and floured 9-inch layer pans. Bake at 350 degrees for 30 to 35 minutes. Cool cake 10 minutes in pans. Remove from pans to wire racks to completely cool. Chill cake before frosting.

CHOCOLATE CREAM FROSTING:

3 squares unsweetened
   chocolate
¼ cup butter

2 cups powdered sugar
½ cup sour cream
2 teaspoons vanilla

In small saucepan, melt chocolate and butter over low heat, stirring to blend. Place powdered sugar in bowl then pour chocolate over; mix well. Add sour cream and vanilla; beat until smooth and creamy.

"A most delectable soft cake."

MARTHA PETERSHEIM, Junction City, OH

Moist Chocolate Cake

2 cups flour
1 teaspoon salt
1 teaspoon baking powder
2 teaspoons baking soda
¾ cup cocoa powder
2 cups sugar

1 cup vegetable oil
1 cup hot coffee
1 cup milk
1 teaspoon vanilla
2 eggs

Sift together flour, salt, baking powder, baking soda, cocoa, and sugar into mixing bowl. Add oil, coffee, and milk; stir well. Add vanilla and eggs. Beat 2 minutes. Batter will be thin. Bake at 325 degrees for 25 to 30 minutes until done.

RUBY BONTRAGER, Lagrange, IN

Amish Dark Chocolate Cake

3 cups sugar
1 cup lard
4 eggs
1 cup cocoa powder
2 teaspoons vanilla

1 cup milk
4 teaspoons baking soda
3⅓ cups flour
1 teaspoon salt
2 cups boiling water

Combine sugar and lard. Add eggs, cocoa, and vanilla; mix well. In separate bowl, mix milk and baking soda. Add milk mixture alternately with flour and salt to first mixture. Add boiling water and mix well. Pour into greased and floured pan. Bake at 350 degrees for 30 minutes or until toothpick comes out clean.

MARY PETERSHEIM, Apple Creek, OH

Never-Fail Red Velvet Cake

2¼ cups sugar
1⅛ cups shortening
3 eggs
3 tablespoons Nesquik chocolate drink mix
3 tablespoons red food coloring

3 tablespoons water
1½ cups buttermilk
3⅜ cups cake flour
¾ teaspoon salt
1½ teaspoons baking soda
1½ teaspoons vinegar

Cream sugar, shortening, and eggs well. Drizzle Nesquik and food coloring into water. Add to creamed mixture. Add buttermilk. Sift flour and salt three times. Add to first mixture. Dissolve baking soda in vinegar. Add to creamed mixture. Spread into greased and floured jelly roll pan. Bake at 350 degrees for 15 to 17 minutes. Do not overbake!

Frosting:

1 cup milk
¼ cup flour
1 cup sugar

1 cup shortening
1 teaspoon vanilla

In saucepan, cook milk and flour until thick. Cool well. In bowl, beat together sugar, shortening, and vanilla. Add flour mixture and beat well.

Jesse and Rose Raber, Montgomery, IN

Zucchini Fudge Cake

4 eggs
2½ cups sugar
2 teaspoons vanilla
¾ cup butter, softened
3 cups flour
½ cup cocoa powder
2 teaspoons baking powder

1 teaspoon baking soda
¾ teaspoon salt
1 cup buttermilk or sour cream
3 cups shredded zucchini
1 cup chopped walnuts

Beat eggs until fluffy. Add sugar. Beat in vanilla and butter. Combine flour, cocoa, baking powder, baking soda, and salt. Add to first mixture with buttermilk. Stir in zucchini and walnuts. Divide batter into four 8- or 9-inch round greased pans. Bake at 350 degrees for 25 to 30 minutes. Cool and frost.

Frosting:

1 cup butter, softened
2 pounds powdered sugar
2 teaspoons vanilla

½ cup milk
½ cup cocoa powder

Blend ingredients until smooth.

John and Kathryn Nisley, Loudonville, OH

Chocolate Chip Coffee Cake

1½ cups flour
¾ cup sugar
2½ teaspoons baking
  powder
¼ teaspoon salt
½ cup mini chocolate chips
¼ cup canola oil

¾ cup milk
1 egg
¾ cup brown sugar
3 teaspoons cinnamon
3 tablespoons butter
¼ cup mini chocolate chips

In bowl, mix flour, sugar, baking powder, salt, and ½ cup chocolate chips. In small bowl, mix oil, milk, and egg. Add to flour mixture and stir until just combined. In small bowl, use your fingers to combine brown sugar, cinnamon, and butter until texture is like coarse sand. Mix in ¼ cup chocolate chips. Spread half of cake batter in 8-inch baking pan sprayed with nonstick spray. Sprinkle with half of topping mixture. Top with remaining batter and sprinkle with remaining topping mixture. Bake at 375 degrees for 25 to 30 minutes.

Esther M. Schwartz, Geneva, IN

Shoofly Cake

4 cups flour
2 cups brown sugar
¾ cup shortening

2 cups boiling water
1 cup molasses
1 tablespoon baking soda

In bowl, mix flour, brown sugar, and shortening until crumbly. Set aside 1 cup. In another bowl, mix boiling water, molasses, and baking soda. Add to first mixture, stirring slightly. Pour into 9x13-inch pan. Sprinkle top with reserved crumbs. Bake at 350 degrees for 40 to 45 minutes or at 300 degrees for 1 hour.

Lena Troyer, Redding, IA
Mary Ellen Wengerd, Campbellsville, KY

Pies

WANDA'S NO-SUGAR APPLE PIE

8 cups sliced Yellow
  Delicious apples
1 can frozen apple juice
  concentrate
2 tablespoons butter
1 teaspoon cinnamon
½ teaspoon nutmeg
4 tablespoons instant
  tapioca
1 baked pie shell

In saucepan, cook apples in apple juice. Add butter, cinnamon, nutmeg, and tapioca. When apples are tender, pour into baked pie shell.

WANDA BRUNSTETTER

CHOCOLATE MOCHA PIE

1 tablespoon gelatin
¼ cup cold water
1 tablespoon cocoa powder
⅛ teaspoon salt
1 teaspoon instant coffee
½ cup sugar
1½ cups milk
1 cup whipped topping
1 teaspoon vanilla
1 baked pie shell

Soften gelatin in cold water. In saucepan, bring to a boil cocoa, salt, coffee, sugar, and milk, stirring constantly. Remove from heat and add gelatin. Cool until slightly thickened. Beat mixture until smooth. In separate bowl, beat whipped topping with vanilla. Fold into cooked mixture. Pour into baked pie shell.

RUBY BONTRAGER, Lagrange, IN

Butterscotch Pie Filling

1 cup brown sugar
1 cup boiling water
½ teaspoon baking soda
Pinch salt
2½ cups water
1 cup sugar

4 tablespoons flour or
  Perma-Flo
3 egg yolks
½ cup water
1 teaspoon vanilla

Boil together brown sugar, 1 cup water, baking soda, and salt. Boil for a while. The longer you boil it, the richer your filling will be. Add 2½ cups water. Blend together sugar, flour, egg yolks, and ½ cup water. Add to pot of sugar water. Boil well until thickened and stir in vanilla.

MRS. YOST (LIZZIE) BORNTRAGER, Bethany, MO

Chocolate Brownie Pie

2 squares unsweetened
  chocolate
2 tablespoons butter
3 large eggs

½ cup sugar
¾ cup dark corn syrup
¾ cup pecans
1 unbaked pie shell

Melt together chocolate and butter. In bowl, mix eggs, sugar, and corn syrup and beat thoroughly. Add to chocolate mixture and beat again. Stir in nuts. Pour into pie shell. Bake at 375 degrees for 40 to 50 minutes.

Lovina M. Schwartz, Geneva, IN

French Silk Pie

½ cup butter
¾ cup sugar
2 squares chocolate, melted

1 teaspoon vanilla
2 eggs
1 baked pie shell

Cream butter and sugar. Add melted chocolate and vanilla. Add 1 egg and beat 5 minutes on high speed. Add second egg and beat 5 minutes. Pour into pie shell and refrigerate.

Rosanna Petersheim, Junction City, OH

Mile-High Chocolate Peanut Butter Pie

1 cup chocolate chips
2 tablespoons butter
3 eggs
¼ cup sugar

¾ cup dark corn syrup
¾ cup chopped pecans
1 unbaked pie shell

Melt chocolate and butter. In bowl, mix eggs, sugar, and corn syrup and beat well. Add to chocolate mixture and beat again. Stir in nuts. Pour into unbaked pie shell. Bake at 375 degrees for 45 to 50 minutes. Cool.

Topping:

1 (8 ounce) package cream
 cheese, divided
1 (8 ounce) carton whipped
 topping, divided

½ cup peanut butter
2 full-size Snickers candy
 bars

Beat 4 ounces cream cheese with 4 ounces whipped topping. In another bowl, beat 4 ounces cream cheese with peanut butter and 4 ounces whipped topping. Spread peanut butter mixture over cooled pie. Then spread on cream cheese mixture. Slice candy bars and place on top.

Susie L. Schwartz, Geneva, IN

Mint Brownie Pie

**6 tablespoons butter (no
substitutes)**
**2 squares unsweetened
chocolate**
1 cup sugar

2 eggs, beaten
½ teaspoon vanilla
½ cup flour

In saucepan, melt butter and chocolate. Stir in sugar until well blended. Add eggs and vanilla; mix well. Stir in flour until well blended. Pour into greased 9-inch springform pan. Bake at 350 degrees for 18 to 20 minutes or until toothpick inserted near center comes out clean. Cool on wire rack.

Filling:

**1 (8 ounce) package cream
cheese, softened**
¾ cup sugar
**½ teaspoon peppermint
extract**
**1 (8 ounce) carton whipped
topping, thawed**

**¼ cup semisweet chocolate
chips**
**Additional whipped topping
and chocolate chips
(optional)**

In mixing bowl, beat cream cheese and sugar until smooth. Add peppermint extract. Fold in whipped topping. Spread evenly over brownie layer. Cover and refrigerate for 1 hour. Remove sides of pan just before serving. Melt chocolate chips and drizzle over top. Garnish with whipped topping and chocolate chips if desired. Yield: 8 servings.

Miriam A. Hershberger, Dalton, OH

Fresh Peach Pie

1 cup sugar	1 cup cream
½ tablespoon flour	5 fresh peaches, peeled
¾ tablespoon instant tapioca	1 unbaked pie shell with top
½ tablespoon cornstarch	Sugar
	Cream

In mixing bowl, combine 1 cup sugar, flour, tapioca, and cornstarch. Add 1 cup cream. Slice peaches into pie shell and dump cream mixture over top. Roll top crust over pie. Cut a few slits in middle of top crust to vent. Dampen edges of crust, cut of excess crust, and crimp edges closed. Blend a little sugar and cream into a glaze and brush over pie. Bake at 350 degrees for 45 minutes.

Martha Petersheim, Junction City, OH

Lemon Meringue Pie

1½ cups water, divided
⅓ cup cornstarch
3 eggs, separated
1½ cups sugar
3 tablespoons butter

¼ cup lemon juice
1 baked pie shell
¼ teaspoon cream of tartar
⅜ cup sugar
1 teaspoon lemon juice

In small bowl, mix ½ cup water, cornstarch, and egg yolks. In saucepan, bring 1½ cups sugar and remaining water to a boil. Quickly stir in cornstarch mixture. Bring to a boil. Remove from heat; add butter and ¼ cup lemon juice. Pour into baked pie shell. To make meringue, beat egg whites and cream of tartar until stiff. Add ⅜ cup sugar and 1 teaspoon lemon juice; beat until glossy. Top pie with meringue; brown.

LOVINA E. HERSHBERGER, Davis City, IA

Old-Fashioned Strawberry Pie

1 cup whole milk
3 egg yolks
1 cup sugar
1 tablespoon cornstarch
½ teaspoon butter

1 teaspoon lemon juice
1 baked pie shell
Fresh strawberries
Egg whites or whipped cream

Cook milk, egg yolks, sugar, cornstarch, butter, and lemon juice in double boiler until thickened. Fill baked pie shell with fresh strawberries. Pour custard mixture over top while still hot. Top with stiffened egg whites and bake as a meringue at 350 degrees for about 10 minutes. Or let custard cool and top with whipped cream.

Elizabeth Byler, New Wilmington, PA

Fresh Fruit Cream Pie

1 cup sugar
1 cup sweet cream
3 tablespoons flour
1 egg, beaten

1 to 2 cups fresh fruit, whole or sliced
1 unbaked pie shell with top

Combine sugar, cream, flour, and egg. Mix well. Place fruit in pie shell. Pour mixture over fruit. Place top crust on and seal edges. Cut vents. Bake at 350 degrees for 45 minutes.

Mary Petersheim, Apple Creek, OH

Aunt Doris's Patted Piecrust

1½ cups flour
1½ teaspoons sugar
1 teaspoon salt

2 teaspoons milk
½ cup vegetable oil

Mix all ingredients to form ball. Pat into pie pan, covering bottom and sides. Bake at 350 degrees for 15 minutes.

Wanda Brunstetter

Piecrust

1 cup butter
½ cup buttermilk

1 egg
1 to 2 cups spelt flour

Mix, adding flour until right consistency to roll out crust. Makes 5 to 6 crusts.

Mrs. Andy A. Hershberger, Navarre, OH

Meringue

5 egg whites (room temperature)
1 teaspoon vanilla

½ teaspoon cream of tartar
12 tablespoons sugar

Beat egg whites, vanilla, and cream of tartar until very stiff. Beat in sugar, 1 tablespoon at a time. Spread meringue over pie filling, sealing to edge of piecrust to prevent shrinkage. Bake according to recipe or until meringue is golden brown—roughly 15 minutes at 350 degrees.

Mrs. Enos Schwartz, Salem, IN

Puddings and Other Desserts

BASIC VANILLA PUDDING

¾ cup sugar
⅓ cup cornstarch
½ teaspoon salt
2 eggs, beaten
½ cup milk
3½ cups milk, scalded

½ teaspoon vanilla
1 tablespoon butter
1 (8 ounce) package cream
    cheese, softened
½ cup powdered sugar
1 carton whipped topping

Mix sugar, cornstarch, and salt. Add eggs and ½ cup milk. Pour into hot milk and stir until it thickens. Add vanilla and butter. Chill. Blend cream cheese and powdered sugar. Fold in whipped topping. Mix with cold pudding.

"Layer in glass bowl with graham crackers and sliced bananas. Delicious!"

MRS. MARIE B. SCHLABACH, Smicksburg, PA

HOMEMADE CHOCOLATE PUDDING

5 cups milk
2 cups sugar
1 cup cornstarch
8 tablespoons cocoa powder

1½ cups milk
5 egg yolks
1 teaspoon vanilla

In saucepan, heat 5 cups milk and sugar. In blender, mix cornstarch, cocoa, 1½ cups milk, and egg yolks. Blend until smooth. Pour into hot milk and cook, stirring constantly. Bring to boiling point but do not boil. Remove from heat and add vanilla.

For pie: pour hot pudding into 2 baked pie shells.

MRS. ENOS SCHWARTZ, Salem, IN

CREAM CHEESE PUDDING

32 graham crackers
¼ cup butter
3 tablespoons sugar
2 packages (⅔ heaping cup) gelatin, any flavor
1 cup boiling water
1 cup cold water
2 (8 ounce) packages cream cheese, softened
2 cups sugar
2 cups cream

Crush graham crackers and mix with butter and 3 tablespoons sugar. Line casserole dish with crumbs, reserving some for garnish. Chill crust. In bowl, mix gelatin into boiling water. Dissolve. Add cold water and refrigerate to cool. In bowl, mix cream cheese and 2 cups sugar. In cold bowl, whip cream. Beat together gelatin and cream cheese mixtures. Add to whipped cream. Spread over crust. Garnish with crumbs. Chill.

MENNO AND ESTHER YODER, Berlin, PA

ROCKY ROAD NO-BAKE CHEESECAKE

3 squares semisweet chocolate
2 (8 ounce) packages cream cheese, softened
⅓ cup sugar
¼ cup milk
2 cups whipped topping, thawed
¾ cup mini marshmallows
⅓ cup chopped peanuts
1 Oreo cookie piecrust

Melt 1 chocolate square as directed on package. Coarsely chop remaining chocolate. In bowl, blend cream cheese, sugar, and milk; mix well. Add melted chocolate; mix well. Whisk in whipped topping until well blended. Stir in chopped chocolate, marshmallows, and nuts. Pour into crust. Refrigerate 4 hours or until set. For garnish, shave additional chocolate on top and dot with mini marshmallows.

ROSANNA PETERSHEIM, Junction City, OH

Apple Dumplings

2 cups flour
2½ teaspoons baking
  powder
½ teaspoon salt

⅔ cup shortening
½ cup milk
6 apples, peeled and halved

Mix flour, baking powder, salt, and shortening until crumbly like pie dough. Add milk. Do not overmix. Roll out dough and cut into 12 squares. Place 1 apple half on each square and wrap with dough. Set dumplings in pan. Pour hot sauce over dumplings. Bake at 350 degrees for 45 minutes or until apples are soft.

Sauce:

2 cups brown sugar
2 cups hot water

½ cup butter
½ teaspoon cinnamon

In saucepan, heat brown sugar, water, butter, and cinnamon until butter is melted and sugar dissolved.

Fannie Miller, Holmesville, OH

BLUEBERRY DESSERT

| ½ cup butter | 1 cup flour |

Mix and bake in 9x13-inch pan for 10 minutes at 350 degrees.

2 (8 ounce) packages reduced fat cream cheese, softened	2 cups nonfat plain Greek yogurt
	⅔ cup powdered sugar
	1 tablespoon lemon juice

Mix and pour on bottom layer. Chill.

TOPPING:

1 cup sugar	1 cup water
3 tablespoons cornstarch	5 cups blueberries, divided
⅛ teaspoon salt	1 tablespoon butter

Mix sugar, cornstarch, salt, water, and 1 cup blueberries. Cook and stir over low heat until thick. Add remaining blueberries and butter. Mix well. Cool. Pour over cream cheese layer.

ESTHER PEACHEY, Fleminsburg, KY

Lemon Lush Dessert

½ cup butter
1 cup flour
½ cup chopped nuts
(optional)
1 cup powdered sugar

1 (8 ounce) package cream
cheese
1¼ cups whipping cream
Lemon pie filling

Mix together butter, flour, and nuts. Press in 9x13-inch pan and bake at 300 degrees for 15 minutes; cool. Combine powdered sugar, cream cheese, and whipping cream. Mix well and spread on top of first mixture. On top of cream cheese mixture, spread lemon pie filling. Cool several hours before serving.

CHARLENE KUEPFER, Milverton, Ontario, Canada

Paradise Dessert

1½ cups crushed graham
crackers
1 tablespoon sugar
2 tablespoons butter,
melted
¼ cup butter
1 egg
1 cup powdered sugar

1 cup cream, whipped
1 cup drained pineapple
1 (8 ounce) package cream
cheese
2 tablespoons sugar
1 teaspoon vanilla
Pinch salt
¼ cup chopped nuts

In bowl, combine crackers, 1 tablespoon sugar, salt, and melted butter. Press into dish, saving some crumbs for garnish. In bowl, cream ¼ cup butter, egg, and powdered sugar. Pour over cracker layer. Chill. In another bowl, mix cream, pineapple, cream cheese, 2 tablespoons sugar, and vanilla. Mix well. Fold in nuts. Spread over other cream layer. Garnish with reserved crumbs.

MARTHA PETERSHEIM, Junction City, OH

Rhubarb Butter Crunch

3 cups diced rhubarb
1 tablespoon spelt flour

1 cup sugar

Mix together and put in baking dish. Then combine:

1 cup oats
1½ cups spelt flour

½ cup brown sugar
¾ cup butter

Put on top of rhubarb. Bake at 375 degrees for 40 minutes or until done.

Lydia Hershberger, Dalton, OH

Caramel Frosting

1 stick butter
1 cup brown sugar

¼ cup or more milk
2 cups powdered sugar

In saucepan, melt butter. Add brown sugar and boil 2 minutes over low heat, stirring constantly. Add milk, continuing to stir until mixture comes to a boil. When cooled, add powdered sugar and stir until smooth.

Note: 1½ batches will cover a cookie sheet of cake or bars.

Regina Bontrager, Lagrange, IN

Peanut Butter Frosting

½ cup creamy peanut butter
5 to 6 tablespoons milk

2 cups powdered sugar
1 teaspoon vanilla

Mix all together until fluffy.

Anita Lorraine Petersheim, Fredericktown, OH

SNACKS AND CANDY

Cheese Ball

4 (8 ounce) packages cream cheese

1 small carton sour cream

2 packages ham or dried beef, diced

Garlic salt to taste

Mix everything together. Serve with crackers.

Ruth Girod, Monroe, IN

Yogurt Sticks

1 cup fruit juice
½ teaspoon vanilla extract

1 cup plain yogurt

Mix ingredients together. Pour into ice tray molds. Insert popsicle sticks and freeze.

Martha Beechy, Butler, Ohio

Black Bean Dip

1 (15 ounce) can black
  beans, rinsed and drained
1 can whole kernel corn,
  drained
1 green or yellow pepper,
  cut up fine

1 mango, peeled and
  chopped
2 plum tomatoes, seeded
  and cut up fine
4 green onions, chopped
2 teaspoons cilantro

Combine in large bowl.

Dressing:

1 package Italian seasoning
⅓ cup red wine vinegar
½ teaspoon salt
½ teaspoon pepper
1 tablespoon lemon juice

½ teaspoon chili pepper
½ teaspoon hot sauce
2 tablespoons water
⅔ cup oil

Blend together. Pour over bean mixture and stir to coat. Refrigerate 1 hour or more. Serve with chips.

Mrs. Velma Schrock, Goshen, IN

Buffalo Chicken Dip

2 cups cooked chicken
2 cups shredded cheese
1 (8 ounce) package cream
  cheese

1 cup ranch dressing
½ cup buffalo sauce

Mix all together and bake at 350 degrees for 30 minutes.

Amanda Rose Esh, Parkesburg, PA

Chicken Dip

4 cups cooked chicken, cut
  up fine
½ cup salsa
1 (8 ounce) package cream
  cheese
1 pound Velveeta cheese

¾ cup chopped onion
1 cup cream of chicken soup
1 cup mayonnaise
½ teaspoon garlic powder
4 ounces green chilies,
  drained

Put all ingredients in slow cooker. Heat on low for at least 1 hour. Serve hot with chips.

Mrs. Velma Schrock, Goshen, IN

Hot Pizza Dip

1 (8 ounce) package cream
  cheese
1 (8 ounce) carton sour
  cream
1 teaspoon oregano

⅛ teaspoon garlic powder
Pinch red pepper
1 cup pizza sauce
½ cup chopped pepperoni

Mix cream cheese, sour cream, oregano, garlic powder, and red pepper. Pour in 9x9-inch pan. Spread with pizza sauce. Top with pepperoni. Bake uncovered at 350 degrees for 20 minutes.

Moses Riehl, Coatsville, PA

Mexican Dip

1 pound ground beef or
  venison
1 small onion, chopped
1 pint salsa
1 small box Velveeta cheese

¼ cup honey
2 teaspoons garlic powder
2 teaspoons salt
1 teaspoon pepper
Hot sauce

Brown beef and onion. Add salsa, cheese, honey, garlic powder, salt, pepper, and several shakes of hot sauce. Stir until cheese melts. Serve hot with tortilla chips.

Lela Brenneman, Montezuma, GA

Sausage Mushroom Appetizers

- 48 large fresh mushrooms
- 2 eggs, lightly beaten
- 1 pound bulk pork sausage, cooked and crumbled
- 1 cup shredded Swiss cheese
- ¼ cup mayonnaise
- 3 tablespoons butter, melted
- 2 tablespoons finely chopped onion
- 2 teaspoons spicy brown or horseradish mustard
- 1 teaspoon garlic salt
- 1 teaspoon Cajun seasoning
- 1 teaspoon Worcestershire sauce

Remove mushroom stems (discard or save for another use). In large bowl, combine eggs, sausage, cheese, mayonnaise, butter, onion, mustard, garlic salt, Cajun seasoning, and Worcestershire sauce. Stuff into mushroom caps. Place in 2 greased 9x13-inch pans. Bake, uncovered, at 350 degrees for 16 to 20 minutes or until heated through.

Mrs. Enos (Maria) Wickey, Monroe, IN

FIBER BALLS

2 cups coconut flakes
3 cups oats
1 cup flaxseed meal
  (optional)
1½ cups peanut butter
1 cup honey

1 tablespoon vanilla
1½ cups chocolate chips
2 tablespoons chia seeds
  (optional)
¾ cup raisins (optional)

Toast coconut flakes in oven until lightly browned. Combine all ingredients and shape into balls.

CHEYANN MILLER, Kalona, IA

FRUIT BALLS

8 ounces pitted dates
1 cup prunes
1 cup walnuts
½ cup dried apricots

⅓ cup raisins
2 tablespoons orange juice
  concentrate
Shredded coconut

Combine dates, prunes, walnuts, apricots, and raisins. Grind or pulse in food processor. Add juice concentrate. Form into small balls. Roll in coconut.

MARY PETERSHEIM, Apple Creek, OH

GRANOLA BARS

4 cups quick oats
5 cups crisped rice cereal
½ cup brown sugar
½ cup honey

1 cup light corn syrup
1½ cups peanut butter
Chocolate chips

In large bowl, mix oats and cereal. In saucepan, bring brown sugar, honey, corn syrup, and peanut butter to a boil. Pour over oat mixture. Press into greased 12x16-inch cookie sheet. Sprinkle with chocolate chips and pat into mixture. Cool before cutting into bars.

MARIETTA BONTRAGER, Ligonier, IN

Monster Cookie Energy Bites

1 cup peanut butter
½ cup honey
3 tablespoons maple syrup
2 teaspoons vanilla
4 tablespoons wheat germ

2 cups oats
⅔ cup ground flaxseeds
2 tablespoons chia seeds
½ cup chocolate chips
½ cup M&M's

Mix all together. Roll into balls. Chill. Can also freeze.

BECKY FISHER, Lancaster, PA

Energy Bars

2 cups butter
3 cups brown sugar
⅔ cup molasses
⅔ cup peanut butter
4 large eggs
3 cups whole wheat flour
2 cups pastry flour
2 cups wheat germ

3 teaspoons baking soda
1 teaspoon salt
1 teaspoon cinnamon
4 cups quick oats
2 cups raisins
2 cups chocolate chips
2 cups chopped nuts

Cream butter, brown sugar, molasses, and peanut butter. Add eggs. In separate bowl, combine whole wheat flour, pastry flour, wheat germ, baking soda, salt, cinnamon, and oats. Add to first mixture. Stir in raisins, chocolate chips, and nuts. Spread into baking pan. Bake at 350 degrees for 20 minutes. These can also be made into cookies.

VERNA STUTZMAN, Navarre, OH

Caramel Corn

2 cups brown sugar	1 teaspoon vanilla
½ cup margarine	½ teaspoon baking soda
½ cup corn syrup	7 quarts popped popcorn
1 teaspoon salt	1 cup peanuts (optional)

In saucepan, bring brown sugar, margarine, corn syrup, and salt to a boil, stirring constantly for 5 minutes. Remove from heat; add vanilla and baking soda. Stir until it looks foamy. Pour over popcorn and peanuts; mix well. Put in large roaster. Bake at 250 degrees for 1 hour, stirring every 15 to 20 minutes. Cool and break apart. Store in airtight container in cool, dry place.

SARAH C.A. SCHWARTZ, Galesburg, KS

CLARA A. YODER, Sugar Grove, PA

LEAH S. YODER, Glenville, PA

BUCKEYE CANDY

1 stick butter, softened	1 pound powdered sugar
1¾ cups creamy peanut butter	1 (12 ounce) package chocolate chips
1 teaspoon vanilla	1 tablespoon shortening

Cream butter, peanut butter, and vanilla. Add powdered sugar until well mixed but not too dry. Roll into 1-inch balls. Place on waxed paper. Melt chocolate chips and shortening over low heat. Use toothpick to pick up and dip each ball three-quarters of the way into chocolate. Return to paper to cool and harden.

EMMA SCHWARTZ, Stanwood, MI

CASHEW CRUNCH

1 pound butter
1 pound sugar

1 pound raw cashews

Cook butter and sugar together over high heat to 248 degrees. Then add cashews and stir until cashews are golden brown. Pour into large greased pan. Let cool then break into pieces.

VERNA STUTZMAN, Navarre, OH

PRALINE PECANS

⅓ cup butter
⅔ cup brown sugar

Dash salt
2 cups chopped pecans

In saucepan, melt butter. Add brown sugar and salt. Heat until it starts bubbling. Mix in pecans. Spread on cookie sheet. Bake at 350 degrees for 5 to 10 minutes, watching closely so they don't get too brown. Stir while cooling.

JUDITH MILLER, Fredericktown, OH

HOMEMADE TWIX BARS

1 box club crackers
½ cup butter
½ cup sugar
¾ cup brown sugar
½ cup milk

1 cup graham cracker
  crumbs
1 cup chocolate chips
¾ cup peanut butter

Line 9x13-inch pan with layer of club crackers. In saucepan, combine butter, sugar, brown sugar, milk, and graham cracker crumbs. Cook 5 minutes, stirring constantly as it will burn easily. Pour over crackers. Add another layer of club crackers. In another saucepan, melt together chocolate chips and peanut butter. Spread on top of crackers. Chill before serving.

MRS. CLEMENS BORNTREGER, Vesper, WI
ELI AND EMMA HERSHBERGER, Canton, PA

Easy Caramels

1 pound butter
2¼ cups brown sugar
Dash salt
1 cup corn syrup

1 (15 ounce) can sweetened
condensed milk
1 teaspoon vanilla
2 teaspoons cream of tartar

In saucepan, melt butter. Add brown sugar and salt, stirring until combined. Blend in corn syrup. Gradually add condensed milk, stirring constantly. Cook and stir over medium heat until candy reaches just past soft ball stage (245 degrees), about 12 to 15 minutes. Remove from heat. Stir in vanilla and cream of tartar. Pour into buttered 9-inch pan. Cool. Cut into small squares and wrap each in waxed paper. For turtles, you can add 3 cups pecans before pouring into pan.

MRS. CLEMENS BORNTREGER, Vesper, WI

CREAM CHEESE FUDGE

3 ounces cream cheese,
softened
2 cups powdered sugar
2 ounces unsweetened
chocolate, melted

¼ teaspoon walnut
flavoring
Dash salt
½ cup chopped nuts

Beat together cream cheese and powdered sugar. Add chocolate and blend. Add flavoring, salt, and nuts. Mix well and press into greased pan. Chill until firm. Cut into squares.

LIZZIE YODER, Fredericksburg, OH

GRANDPA'S FUDGE

½ cup butter
4½ cups sugar
1 can evaporated milk
1 cup marshmallow crème
1 (13 ounce) bar sweetened
chocolate, grated

2 (12 ounce) packages
chocolate chips
2 teaspoons vanilla
2 cups walnuts, coarsely
chopped

Combine butter, sugar, and milk. Cook for 5½ minutes, stirring constantly. Remove from heat. Add marshmallow crème, grated chocolate, chocolate chips, and vanilla. Beat until well mixed then add nuts. Beat until well mixed and smooth. Pour into buttered 9x13-inch pan. Cool until firm then cut. Yield: 5 pounds.

RACHEL SCHLABACH, Millersburg, OH

Healthy Peanut Butter Fudge

1 cup coconut oil, melted
1 cup peanut butter
1 cup ground flax or oats
⅓ cup honey

½ cup cocoa powder
½ teaspoon salt
1 scoop protein powder (optional)

Mix everything together, press into pan, and chill.

MARYANN STAUFFER, Homer City, PA

Never-Fail Fudge

1 cup sugar
1 cup brown sugar
¼ cup butter
¼ cup corn syrup

½ cup cream
1 heaping tablespoon peanut butter

In saucepan, combine sugar, brown sugar, butter, corn syrup, and cream. Cook to soft ball stage. Watch carefully. As soon as mixture forms a soft ball when dropped in cold water, remove from heat and add peanut butter. Beat until it begins to thicken. Pour into buttered pan and cut before it cools completely.

MRS. ELLA ARLENE YODER, Arcola, IL

DAIRY PRODUCTS

Cottage Cheese

1 gallon milk
½ cup vinegar
1 (16 ounce) carton sour
  cream

Milk
Salt to taste

Heat 1 gallon milk to 180 degrees. Add vinegar and stir until whey separates. Let stand 1 minute. Pour into fine mesh colander. Rinse curds with cold water. In bowl, finely chop curds. Add sour cream, enough milk to thin to preference, and salt.

AMANDA BYLER, Curwensville, PA

Homemade Cottage Cheese

5 gallons skimmed milk
¼ tablet rennet or 2½
  tablespoons liquid rennet
¼ cup cold water

5 teaspoons coarse salt
2 tablespoons sugar
Cream

Heat milk to 72 degrees. In small bowl, put rennet in water, stirring until dissolved. Add to milk. Let sit covered 1 to 2 hours until milk has a clean break. Cut milk in ½-inch cubes. Slowly heat milk to 100 degrees. Drain and wash curds. Add salt and sugar. When ready to eat, add cream to taste preference.

MARTHA PETERSHEIM, Junction City, OH

CREAM CHEESE

5 quarts milk
1 cup sugar
¾ teaspoon salt
1 cup yogurt

Bring milk, sugar, and salt to a boil and boil hard for 2 minutes. Add yogurt, stirring well. Keep warm until set thick. Drain in cheesecloth for 24 hours. Place in covered bowl for 24 hours before using.

DORCAS MARIE YODER, Meyersdale, PA

DELICIOUS CREAM CHEESE

2 quarts milk
½ cup yogurt starter or yogurt
   with live and active yeast culture
Salt to taste

Heat milk to 180 degrees. Cool to 120 degrees then add yogurt starter, beating mixture well with egg beater. Cover and let sit in warm place for 4 hours. Drain in cheesecloth or put clean cloth in colander and drain overnight or longer. Add salt and whip with spoon or ladle until smooth and shiny.

MENNO AND ESTHER YODER, Berlin, PA

Delicious Hard Cheese Curds

4 gallons milk
4 to 5 ounces culture (e.g., buttermilk)
1 teaspoon rennet

½ cup water
4 tablespoons salt
½ teaspoon cheese coloring (optional)

Heat milk to 88 to 90 degrees. Add culture. Mix well. In cup, combine rennet and water. Add to milk. Stir no longer than 1 minute. Let stand 30 minutes to 1 hour. Cut through with long knife. Heat on high, stirring constantly until it reaches 98 to 100 degrees (no higher). Remove from heat and let sit 10 to 15 minutes. Pour off whey. Break up curds and mix in salt and coloring. Dump in cheesecloth-lined mold—do not press.

For pressed, hard sliceable cheese: After 1 hour draining in cloth, flip cheese upside down and let sit in mold for 24 hours. Remove from mold. Keep at room temperature for 1 week, turning cheese daily. Store in cool place. Usually ready in 2 weeks.

Lena Troyer, Redding, IA

ANNA'S HOMEMADE CHEESE

Milk (any amount)
1 teaspoon baking soda for
    every 3 cups curds
Salt to taste

¼ cup butter
Cheddar cheese
½ cup cream (optional)

Set milk out to sour until thick. In pan, heat milk until it feels hot to touch. Strain through cheesecloth, draining very well. Wash curds three to four times in strong salted water. Drain off water. Add baking soda, salt, butter, and cheese. For softer cheese, add cream and melt in double boiler, stirring often. Enjoy cheese with crackers.

MRS. DAVID J. KURTZ, Smicksburg, PA

"VELVEETA" CHEESE

1 gallon milk
2 teaspoons citric acid
1 teaspoon baking soda
¼ cup butter

1 teaspoon salt
3 tablespoons cheddar
    cheese powder
½ cup milk

Heat 1 gallon milk to 140 degrees. Remove from heat and add citric acid. Stir gently until milk separates. Drain off whey. Rinse curds with cold water and drain for 30 to 40 minutes. Add baking soda, butter, salt, cheese powder, and ½ cup milk. Heat in double boiler, stirring briskly until lumps dissolve. More or less milk may be added for softer or harder cheese. Cheese may be put through cheesecloth or strainer after melting. Refrigerate to harden.

MARYANN STAUFFER, Homer City, PA
BARBIE S. WENGERD, Thompsontown, PA

CHEESE CRUMBS

3 gallons skimmed milk
⅛ teaspoon cottage cheese culture

Warm milk to 72 degrees. Add culture, mixing thoroughly. Cover and let stand 16 to 24 hours or until set. Cut into ¼-inch cubes or use wire whisk to stir and cut. Don't stir too much. Heat to 130 to 120 degrees, stirring occasionally. Drain in cheesecloth or clean pillowcase. Hang to drain for about 8 hours or overnight.

EMMA BEILER, Delta, PA

FARMERS HARD CHEESE

4 gallons milk
¼ teaspoon cheese culture
½ teaspoon rennet

½ cup cold water
4 tablespoons salt

Heat milk to 90 degrees or use fresh warm milk. Add culture. Mix rennet and water; add to milk. Let sit 30 minutes to 1 hour. Cut curds with knife. Heat on high to 100 degrees. Let sit 15 minutes. Pour off whey. Add salt. Pour into mold. No need to press.

SARAH BEILER, Doylesburg, PA

Muenster Cheese #1

2½ gallons milk
2 teaspoons baking soda
½ cup butter

1½ teaspoons salt
2 cups cream

Let milk sit out on counter to sour and thicken (not too sour). Put in large kettle and heat to 150 degrees. Pour into cheesecloth. Squeeze out whey and let hang overnight until curds are dry. Crumble curds and mix in baking soda, butter, and salt. Mix very well with hands. Let sit in warm place for 2 hours. Put curds in double boiler and add cream; stir until melted. Pour into mold or deep pan. Chill. Great sliced for toasted cheese. I like to use a bit less cream for easy slicing. You can use more cream for a smear cheese.

MRS. ELI A. KURTZ, Dayton, PA

Muenster Cheese #2

2 gallons fresh whole milk
½ cup butter
2 teaspoons baking soda
1 teaspoon salt

1 tablespoon cheese powder
1 cup hot milk
2 cups sour cream, divided
1 cup mayonnaise

Let fresh milk sit a day or two in warm place until it is thick and quite firm. Stir and heat until it is too hot to put your hand in (125 to 150 degrees). Pour into cheesecloth bag and allow to drain 12 hours or overnight. In saucepan, combine curds, butter, baking soda, salt, and cheese powder. Set for 2 hours. Add hot milk*, 1 cup sour cream, and mayonnaise. Stir until smooth and melted over low heat. Remove from heat. Add 1 cup sour cream. Pour into buttered dish. Chill.

*If curds are not dry, omit hot milk.

DAVID AND LYDIA BONTRAGER, Kidder, MO

Mozzarella Cheese #1

2 gallons whole milk
2½ teaspoons citric acid
   powder
½ cup cool water

½ teaspoon liquid rennet
½ cup cool water
1 gallon water
2 teaspoons salt

Use heavy saucepan for milk. Dissolve citric acid in ½ cup cool water. Add to milk and stir. Heat milk to 88 degrees. Add rennet to ½ cup cool water. Stir into milk mixture for 15 seconds. Let sit 15 minutes to coagulate. Cut curds into ½-inch cubes and let rest 5 minutes. Over low heat, stir gently and bring temperature to 108 degrees. Stir often to separate curds. Hold at 108 degrees for 35 minutes. Drain in colander 15 minutes. Heat 1 gallon water to 170 degrees. Add salt. Tear cheese into 6 to 8 strips and put in water. With large spoon, press cheese up sides until it softens and globs together. Stretch until opaque and shiny. Drain and cool. Eat now, refrigerate, or freeze.

Laura Miller, Fredericktown, OH

Mozzarella Cheese #2

2½ gallons milk
2 cups vinegar
2 teaspoons salt

2 teaspoons baking soda
½ cup butter

Heat milk to 126 degrees. Stir in vinegar until you see curdles. Let sit undisturbed off heat for 1 hour. Pour or ladle into cheesecloth and squeeze out whey. Wash curds in cold water and squeeze out water. The harder you squeeze, the harder the final cheese will be. Mix salt and baking soda into curds and let sit 30 minutes. In heavy saucepan, heat butter and curds, stirring to melt curds. Curds will bind and form a smooth rope. Put cheese in mold. (Susan says, "I use an empty yogurt container.")

Mrs. Levi Shrock, Ashland, OH

Susan Zook, Apple Creek, OH

Anna's Yogurt

1 gallon skimmed milk
2 tablespoons unflavored
  gelatin
1 cup water

2 cups sugar (optional)
2 teaspoons vanilla
4 tablespoons yogurt
  starter

Heat milk to 150 degrees; cool to 130 degrees. Dissolve gelatin in water. Add gelatin and sugar to milk. Add vanilla and yogurt starter; beat well. Pour into 5 quart jars; place lids on jars but do no screw down. Put where temperature is 85 degrees for 8 hours. Oven is fine in winter, or ice chest with warmed water nearly up to top of jars will work. Store in refrigerator.

"We make good smoothies with homemade yogurt by putting frozen fruit, yogurt, maple syrup, and a pinch of salt in a blender. Blend until smooth."

ANNA R. WENGERD, Thompsontown, PA

Delicious Yogurt

1 gallon milk
2 tablespoons unflavored gelatin
½ cup cold water
½ cup plain yogurt
2 teaspoons vanilla (optional)

1 cup maple syrup or ¼ cup xylitol or ½ cup sugar (optional)
Pie filling or flavoring of choice

Heat milk to 180 degrees. Let cool to 130 degrees. Soak gelatin in water. Add soaked gelatin, yogurt, vanilla, and maple syrup to milk. Beat all together and set in oven with pilot light on for 8 hours. Skim off skin on top and beat well. Add pie filling. Chill. Beat well before serving and you will have delicious smooth yogurt. Store in refrigerator.

Note from MaryAnn: When I make my yogurt, I use an insulated cooler. Fill it with hot water. Divide milk mixture in jars and set them in the water for several hours. When a knife inserted in the yogurt comes out clean, it is done. Sometimes I let it sit overnight. I found this useful as I don't have a pilot light. I like the results I get.

From Linda: *"Mine sets best when I use organic yogurt for starter. Freeze ½ cup of your yogurt before adding pie filling to use for your next batch."*

Linda Burkholder, Fresno, OH
MaryAnn Kempf, Winterset, IA
Ella Schlabach, Bellville, OH
Barbara Yoder, Gilman, WI

Maple Yog

1 gallon milk, less ¾ cup reserved
½ cup sugar
¾ cup maple syrup

1 tablespoon maple flavoring
½ cup tapioca starch
⅛ teaspoon yogurt culture

Heat milk to 170 degrees. Add sugar and maple syrup, stirring until dissolved. Add maple flavoring. Mix tapioca starch with reserved ¾ cup milk; add to warm milk mixture. Cool to 110 degrees, then add yogurt culture. Mix well and put into oven overnight. (Must have either a pilot light or lightbulb.) The next morning, mix well and refrigerate.

Ruby Stoltzfus, New Holland, PA

MARTHA'S YOGURT

1 tablespoon unflavored
  gelatin
¼ cup cold water

2 quarts milk
1 cup plain yogurt

Soak gelatin in water. In saucepan, heat milk to 185 degrees. Add soaked gelatin; stir well. Cool back down to 110 to 115 degrees. Add yogurt, stirring well. Put in oven with pilot light on or in other warm spot for 7 to 8 hours. Beat well, put in jars with lids, and refrigerate. Remember to always save 1 cup for your next batch.

Variation: we like whipping in flavored gelatin or Kool-Aid and adding fresh fruit.

Sour Cream Substitution: Do everything the same as instructions for yogurt, except use sour cream instead of yogurt for starter. You can also replace milk with cream.

MARTHA PETERSHEIM, Junction City, OH

HOMEMADE GREEK YOGURT

1 gallon milk
¾ cup Greek yogurt

⅓ cup honey
1½ tablespoons vanilla

Heat milk to 190 degrees. Remove from heat. Submerge pot into cold water. Cool milk to 130 degrees. Add yogurt to cooled milk. Put covered milk mixture into oven overnight. Next morning, put it into strainer lined with cheesecloth. Let drain for 4 to 5 hours. Let the whey drain into your sink. Flip into bowl. Add honey and vanilla.

LINDA BURKHOLDER, Fresno, OH

Vanilla Yogurt

1 gallon milk
2 cups sugar
2 tablespoons unflavored
  gelatin

1 cup water
2 teaspoons vanilla
¼ cup plain yogurt

Heat milk to 190 degrees. Cool to 130 degrees. Add sugar. Dissolve gelatin in water. Add to milk. Add vanilla and yogurt. Beat with beater until well mixed. Pour into 5 quart jars. Cover, but don't tighten lids. Place somewhere that is around 85 degrees for 8 hours. Or place jars in warm water in ice chest for 8 hours. Then refrigerate. Before serving, you may add any kind of fruit.

Katie R. Hostetler, Smicksburg, PA

Fast Soft Goat Cheese

1 gallon fresh goat milk
½ cup apple cider vinegar

1 tablespoon salt

After chilling fresh milk, heat on stove to 90 degrees. Stir gently for 2 to 3 minutes and remove from heat. Add vinegar and continue to stir gently until soft curds form. Pour into cheesecloth-lined colander resting in stainless-steel bowl. Let rest for 2 minutes, then lift cheesecloth with curds above colander. Gently squeeze to remove whey. Empty curds into glass or stainless-steel bowl. Add salt and mix together with clean hands. Form curds into ball or log, wrap in plastic wrap, and store in refrigerator for at least 2 days before eating. Enjoy!

Elizabeth Byler, New Wilmington, PA

Cottage Cheese from Goat's Milk

1 gallon goat milk (2 or more days old)

Set milk out on countertop until clabbered (separated). Pour into 12x17-inch cake pan. Put into oven at 200 degrees for 1 hour. Turn off oven and leave for another hour. Drain through cheesecloth. Refrigerate.

MaryAnn Kempf, Winterset, IA

Goat Yogurt

2½ tablespoons unflavored gelatin
½ cup water
1 gallon goat milk

1⅓ cups sugar
½ cup yogurt starter
1 teaspoon vanilla

Soak gelatin in water. Heat milk to 200 degrees. Add gelatin and sugar. Beat. Cool to 125 degrees. Add starter and vanilla. Put in unheated oven for 9 to 11 hours.

Crystal Ropp, Kalona, IA

Simple Delicious Ice Cream

7 eggs, beaten well
4 cups cream
2½ cups brown sugar

1 tablespoon vanilla or
   other flavoring of choice
Milk

Blend eggs, cream, brown sugar, and vanilla. Pour into 6-quart ice cream freezer. Top with milk to three-quarters full. Freeze and enjoy.

Note: this recipe uses raw eggs.

LEVI D. STOLTZFUS, Willow Hill, PA

Quick Ice Cream

8 large eggs
1 heaping cup sugar
1 quart cream

2 tablespoons vanilla
2 teaspoons maple flavoring

Beat eggs until very light and foamy. Add sugar and cream; beat hard. Pour mixture into ice cream freezer can to within 4 inches from top, then fill rest of can with milk. Add flavorings.

Notes: Recipe is for 1-gallon ice cream freezer. If chocolate flavor is desired, add 2 tablespoons chocolate syrup to sugar. This recipe uses raw eggs.

VALERIE BORNTRAGER, Kalona, IA

Honey Ice Cream

2 quarts milk, less ½ cup
  reserved
10 eggs, separated
3 tablespoons unflavored
  gelatin, soaked in a little
  water

1½ cups honey
2 teaspoons instant coffee
2 teaspoons stevia
2 teaspoons vanilla
2 quarts heavy cream

Heat milk in saucepan. Beat egg whites stiff then add ½ cup reserved milk. When milk in pot is boiling, add egg whites. Remove from heat and add soaked gelatin. Stir well. Add honey, coffee, stevia, and vanilla. Cool. Before freezing, whip cream and whip egg yolks; add to first mixture. Pour into 2-gallon ice cream freezer and add enough milk to fill. Freeze according to manufacturer's directions.

Notes: If cooled quickly, ice cream tends to have a better flavor. Adding honey with stevia when cooking or baking gives a honey sweetness with no stevia aftertaste.

Mrs. Wilmer Beachy, Laurelville, OH

"Dairy Queen" Ice Cream

2 tablespoons gelatin
½ cup cold water
4 cups milk
2 cups sugar

2 teaspoons vanilla
1 teaspoon salt
3 cups cream

Soak gelatin in water. In saucepan, heat milk until hot but not boiling. Remove from heat. Add gelatin, sugar, vanilla, and salt. Allow to cool. Add cream. Put in refrigerator for 5 to 6 hours to chill before freezing in ice cream freezer. Yield: 1 gallon.

Dorcas Marie Yoder, Meyersdale, PA

Chocolate Chip Ice Cream

3½ to 4 squares
  unsweetened chocolate
  (about 4 ounces)
4 teaspoons butter

2 tablespoons sugar
Your favorite vanilla ice
  cream recipe

In saucepan over low heat, melt together chocolate, butter, and sugar. Pour into partly frozen ice cream while turning paddles. Finish freezing process.

EMMA SCHWARTZ, Stanwood, MI

Frozen Yogurt

1 quart milk
1 cup sugar
2 eggs
1 box instant vanilla
  pudding mix

2 quarts homemade yogurt
2 cups whipped topping
1 quart thick red raspberry
  puree

Heat milk and sugar, stirring to dissolve sugar. Cool. Beat eggs and add pudding mix. Add to cooled milk. Add yogurt, whipped topping, and raspberry puree. Pour in ice cream freezer and freeze according to manufacturer's directions.

Note: this recipe uses raw eggs.

ESTHER RABER, Millersburg, OH

Ice Cream Bars

2 cups heavy cream
1 teaspoon vanilla
1 cup sugar or ½ cup maple
   syrup

6 eggs, separated
Wafers or graham crackers

Beat cream with vanilla and sugar until stiff. Beat egg yolks and egg whites in separate bowls until very stiff. Fold together cream, egg yolks, and egg whites. Put wafers on bottom of cake or sheet pan, pour mixture on top of wafers, then put another layer of wafers on top of cream mixture. Freeze.

Note: this recipe uses raw eggs.

HENRY AND FANNIE HERTZLER, Bloomsburg, PA

MISCELLANEOUS THINGS

Kitchen Pantry

Ice Cream Topping

1 (12 ounce) package
chocolate chips

½ cup crunchy peanut
butter
1 stick butter

In saucepan, melt together chocolate chips, peanut butter, and butter. Stir until well combined. Cool. Do not refrigerate. Serve over ice cream. It will harden when it chills.

Ruby Bontrager, Lagrange, IN

Hard Shell Ice Cream Sauce

¼ cup butter
3 tablespoons milk

1 cup chocolate chips

In saucepan, heat butter and milk, stirring well until butter melts. Add chocolate chips. Stir until smooth. Serve lukewarm—sauce will harden on top of ice cream. If you refrigerate sauce, it will harden and need to be warmed.

Judith Miller, Fredericktown, OH

Chocolate Syrup

1 cup corn syrup
2 tablespoons cocoa powder
6 tablespoons sugar

1 teaspoon vanilla
2 teaspoons butter
Dash salt

In saucepan, mix all ingredients together and heat to boiling point, but don't let it boil. Take off heat. Good served warm over ice cream, or use to make chocolate milk.

Sarah C.A. Schwartz, Galesburg, KS

Pear Butter

1 gallon ground pears
5 pounds sugar
1 pint corn syrup

Few drops orange oil
(optional)

Cook pears and sugar until thick. Add corn syrup and orange oil. Put into jars and seal.

Mrs. Emanuel J. Swartzentruber, Navarre, OH

Green Tomato Jelly

4 cups chopped green
tomatoes
4 cups sugar

2 teaspoons lemon juice
2 small packages black
raspberry gelatin

Combine tomatoes, sugar, and lemon juice in saucepan. Cook 20 minutes. Remove from heat. Add gelatin. Put in jars.

"The tomato seeds make it look like blackberries!"

Joanna Miller, Loudonville, OH

Grape Molasses

1½ cups pure grape juice
4 cups sugar

½ gallon corn syrup

Cook grape juice and sugar on medium heat for 5 minutes until sugar is well dissolved. Add corn syrup and cook 2 minutes. Can also use elderberry juice in place of grape juice.

Mrs. Emanuel J. Swartzentruber, Navarre, OH

Apple Butter

16 cups applesauce
3 pounds brown sugar
1 cup apple cider vinegar

1 teaspoon salt
2 tablespoons cinnamon

Mix all ingredients and put in casserole dish. Bake at 350 degrees for 3 hours, stirring occasionally. You can add more sugar if not sweet enough. If not thick enough, bake longer. Then pour into jars and seal.

Elizabeth Byler, Milton, PA

Not-Too-Sweet Pancake Syrup

½ cup sugar
1 tablespoon Perma-Flo
2 cups boiling water
3 tablespoons brown sugar

4 tablespoons butter
⅛ teaspoon salt
1 teaspoon vanilla
1 teaspoon maple flavoring

In saucepan, combine sugar and Perma-Flo with a little cold water. Gradually add boiling water. Cook until clear. Add brown sugar, butter, salt, vanilla, and maple flavoring, stirring until sugar and butter melt.

Emme D. Byler, New Wilmington, PA

Homemade "Honey"

5 pounds sugar
1½ pints water

1 teaspoon alum
85 red clover blossoms

In saucepan, bring sugar and water to a boil. Boil until water is clear (about 1 minute). Add alum and boil for 2 minutes. Remove from heat. Add clover blossoms. Let stand 10 minutes. Strain. Good on things like pancakes.

ANNA HERSHBERGER, Fredericksburg, OH

Dutch Honey

2 cups brown sugar
1 heaping tablespoon flour

¾ cup cream or evaporated milk
½ cup butter

Mix brown sugar and flour. Add with cream and butter to saucepan and bring to a boil. Delicious served warm on waffles and pancakes.

ANNA BYLER, Spartansburg, PA

Marshmallow Crème Fluff

⅓ cup water
¾ cup sugar
¾ cup corn syrup

3 large egg whites, room temperature
½ teaspoon cream of tartar
1 teaspoon vanilla

In medium saucepan, combine water, sugar, and corn syrup. Insert candy thermometer and heat over medium heat. Do not stir or crystals will form. When it reaches about 225 degrees, start whipping egg whites and cream of tartar to stiff peaks. Check sugar mixture, which should now be 240 degrees. Remove from heat and pour with a slow and steady stream into stiff egg whites. Turn mixer on medium-high speed and mix for about 7 to 8 minutes or until mixture is thick and glossy. Add vanilla. Will keep 2 weeks at room temperature. Better than store-bought. Delicious on toast instead of jelly.

SUSAN YODER, Butler, OH

Fruit Glaze

3 cups water
2 cups pineapple juice
1½ cups sugar

½ cup Perma-Flo or other thickener
⅓ cup apricot or peach gelatin

In saucepan, heat water and pineapple juice. In bowl, combine sugar, Perma-Flo, and gelatin. Add enough water to make a paste. Stir into juice and boil until thickened. Remove from heat and cool. Add fruit of your choice. Recipe makes enough glaze for a large pail of mixed fruit.

NEVA HERSHBERGER, Apple Creek, OH

STRAWBERRY FREEZER JAM

**3 cups crushed
strawberries, divided
4 cups sugar**

**1 tablespoon lemon juice
1 package powdered fruit
pectin**

In 4-quart pot, combine 2 cups strawberries, sugar, and lemon juice. Let stand 10 minutes. In saucepan, mix pectin with remaining 1 cup strawberries. Bring to a boil, stirring constantly. Boil hard for 1 minute. Immediately stir pectin mixture into fruit, stirring for 3 minutes. Fill jars or other containers, cover, and let sit at room temperature for 24 hours. Store jam in freezer. It keeps in refrigerator for about 3 weeks. Yield: 4½ to 5 cups.

"This is our favorite freezer jam. It has a rich fruity flavor. Also good made with raspberries."

ANITA LORRAINE PETERSHEIM, Fredericktown, OH

TACO SEASONING

9 teaspoons chili powder
9 teaspoons paprika
13½ teaspoons cumin
18 teaspoons parsley flakes

9 teaspoons onion powder
4½ teaspoons garlic salt
4½ teaspoons oregano

Mix and store in airtight container. Seven teaspoons mix equals 1 store-bought package.

LINDA BURKHOLDER, Fresno, OH

BBQ Sauce

1 cup Perma-Flo
15 cups tomato juice
4 cups ground onion
¾ cup lemon juice
⅔ cup sugar
⅛ teaspoon paprika
2 bottles Worcestershire
  sauce

3 cups vinegar
8 cups brown sugar
½ cup yellow mustard
⅔ cup liquid smoke
⅔ cup salt

Mix Perma-Flo with a little tomato juice to create a paste; set aside. In large pot, stir together all ingredients (except Perma-Flo paste); bring to a boil. Add Perma-Flo paste and mix well. Pour into jars and cold pack for 10 minutes.

WILLIAM AND REBECCA TROYER, Navarre, OH

Herb Salt

1 cup dried and ground
  herbs (e.g., combination of
  alfalfa, clove, dandelion,
  celery leaves, chives,
  onion, garlic, etc.)

1 cup salt
1 cup water

Use herbs of your choice. Mix herbs, salt, and water together and let stand on counter for 1 week. Put on cookie sheet and dry thoroughly. Crumble fine with rolling pin.

EMMA BEILER, Delta, PA

Thick and Chunky Salsa

14 pounds tomatoes, cut up
5 cups chopped onion
10 green peppers, chopped
1 cup vinegar
¼ cup salt
1 teaspoon garlic powder

2 teaspoons chili powder
2 teaspoons oregano
1 package Mrs. Wages salsa mix
10 tablespoons Clear Jel

Mix all ingredients except Clear Jel in large pot. Boil for 45 minutes. Mix Clear Jel with a little water until smooth. Add to salsa and mix well. Return to a boil. Fill jars and cold pack for 20 minutes. Yield: 16 pints.

VERNA STUTZMAN, Navarre, OH

Canned Tomato Soup

½ pound tomatoes, made into juice
10 onions, chopped
2 bunches celery, chopped

2 handfuls fresh parsley, chopped
1 pound carrots, chopped
Salt and pepper to taste
Seasonings of choice

Put juice in large kettle or cold packer. Add vegetables and seasonings. Bring to a boil, then cook on low heat for 2 hours. Put in jars and seal in water bath.

LYDIA HERSHBERGER, Dalton, OH

Pizza Sauce

1 quart chopped onion
10 green peppers
¼ cup hot peppers
Sauté vegetables in 1 cup butter
12 quarts tomato juice

4 pounds sugar
4 heaping teaspoons oregano
4 teaspoons garlic powder
4 teaspoons salt
1½ teaspoons cloves

Boil in open kettle for 1½ hours. Thicken with Clear Jel.

SARAH BEILER, Doylesburg, PA

MANDY'S SPAGHETTI SAUCE

½ bushel tomatoes
3 large onions
1 bunch celery
4 bell peppers
2 hot peppers
⅔ cup salt
2 teaspoons pepper

3 teaspoons garlic salt
2 teaspoons Worcestershire sauce
1 cup vegetable oil
2 cups sugar
1 quart tomato paste

Process tomatoes through sieve. Chop vegetables. In large pot, combine tomatoes, vegetables, salt, pepper, garlic salt, Worcestershire sauce, oil, and sugar. Cook until thickened. Add tomato paste and simmer 30 minutes. Pour into jars and seal in water bath.

MRS. LEVI HERSHBERGER, Homerville, OH

Vegetable Broth

2 large potatoes, chopped
1 cup shredded carrots
1 cup chopped celery stalks
  and leaves
1 medium onion, chopped
2 to 3 cloves garlic

1 cup greens (parsley, wheat
  grass, lettuce, turnip
  greens, alfalfa)
Dash cayenne pepper
6 cups water

Place ingredients in pot. Cook over low heat for 30 minutes. Let sit off heat for 30 minutes. Strain and serve. If not used immediately, store in refrigerator and use within 1 week.

Note: do not use spinach or vegetables from the cabbage family as they are too acidic.

This is an alkaline-cleansing, mineral-rich drink that has been used to help treat disease. Also good for lactating mothers.

MRS. LEVI HERSHBERGER, Homerville, OH

Sauerkraut

20 pounds cabbage
¾ cup salt

Remove outer leaves and any undesirable portions from firm, mature heads of cabbage. Wash and drain. Cut into halves or quarters. Remove core. Use food processor or sharp knife to cut cabbage into thin shreds, about 1/16-inch thick.

Combine 5 pounds shredded cabbage with 2½ tablespoons salt in large bowl, mixing thoroughly. Let stand for several minutes to wilt slightly; this allows packing without excessive breaking or bruising of shreds. Pack salted cabbage firmly and evenly into large, clean pickling container. Use wooden spoon, tamper, or hands to press down firmly until juices come to surface.

Repeat shredding, salting, wilting, and packing cabbage until container is filled to within 3 to 4 inches from top. If juice does not cover cabbage, add brine. To make brine, combine 1½ tablespoons salt to 1 quart water. Bring to a boil. Cool.

Cover cabbage with muslin or cheesecloth and tuck edges down against inside of container. Weight cabbage under brine. Formation of gas bubbles indicates fermentation is taking place. Remove and discard scum formation each day. Store container in cool place. Full fermentation usually takes 3 to 6 weeks.

WILLIAM AND REBECCA TROYER, Navarre, OH

Canned Red Beets

Soft red beets   **Vinegar**
Sugar   **Red beet juice or water**
Salt

Fill jars with beets. To each quart, add ¾ scant cup sugar, 1 teaspoon salt, and ¼ cup vinegar. Fill jars with beet juice. Seal with 2-piece lid and boil jars 30 minutes.

Sarah Beiler, Doylesburg, PA

Refrigerator Pickles

6 cups sliced cucumbers
1 cup sliced onion
1 cup sliced green pepper
2 tablespoons salt

2 cups sugar
1 tablespoon celery seed
1 cup vinegar

Mix all together. Store in refrigerator. Ready in 24 hours. Will keep up to 1 year.

IRENE A. SCHWARTZ, Monroe, IN

Pickle Relish

3½ cups shredded, unpeeled
    cucumbers
6 medium carrots,
    shredded
2 medium onions, minced
2 tablespoons salt

1½ cups vinegar
½ cup water
2½ cups sugar
1½ teaspoons celery seed
1½ teaspoons mustard seed

Mix cucumbers, carrots, onions, and salt. Let stand 3 hours; drain. In saucepan, bring vinegar, water, sugar, celery seed, and mustard seed to a boil. Add vegetable mixture and simmer 20 minutes. Put in jars and seal in water bath.

MRS. IVAN C. SCHROCK, Jamesport, MO

Garlic Spread

1 cup butter, softened
4 tablespoons mayonnaise
6 cloves garlic, minced
4 teaspoons oregano

2 teaspoons salt
2 teaspoons pepper
½ teaspoon sage (optional)

Mix all together. Spread on slice of bread and toast, or serve on sandwiches. It takes only a thin layer to give lots of flavor!

MARY KING, Kinzers, PA

Homemade Mustard

5 cups water
5 cups sugar
5 eggs
2½ cups vinegar
6 heaping tablespoons flour

5 heaping tablespoons dry mustard
1 teaspoon turmeric
¾ teaspoon salt

Bring water to a boil. Beat all other ingredients together to make a paste. Add paste to boiling water. Stirring constantly, boil until thick, about 10 minutes.

CHARLENE KUEPFER, Milverton, Ontario, Canada

Sandwich Spread

12 red bell peppers	4 onions
12 green bell peppers	1 hot pepper
12 green tomatoes	1 pint sweet pickles

Grind bell peppers, tomatoes, onions, hot pepper, and pickles with fine blade. Pour boiling water over pepper mixture to cover. Let stand 5 minutes. Drain.

Dressing:

3½ cups sugar	½ cup flour
1 cup vinegar	Cold water
3½ teaspoons salt	1 quart Miracle Whip salad dressing
1 small jar prepared mustard	

In saucepan, combine sugar, vinegar, salt, and mustard. Boil for 15 minutes. In small bowl, combine flour and water to make a paste. Slowly add to hot mixture and cook until slightly thickened. Remove from heat. Add salad dressing. Whip well. Seal in pint jars. I cook jars in a water bath for 10 minutes.

Mrs. Ella Arlene Yoder, Arcola, IL

Cheese Sauce

2 tablespoons butter
2 tablespoons flour
2 cups milk, divided

1 cup diced Velveeta cheese
½ teaspoon salt

In saucepan, melt butter. Stir in flour and 1 cup milk. Stir to remove lumps and cook for a couple of minutes to thicken. Add remaining 1 cup milk, cheese, and salt, stirring until cheese is melted.

Mrs. Reuben (Martha) Byler, Atlantic, PA

Mac Sauce

⅓ cup creamy french
 dressing
1 cup Miracle Whip salad
 dressing
¼ cup pickle relish

1½ teaspoons minced onion
1 tablespoon sugar
¼ teaspoon pepper

Mix together and serve with grilled hamburgers.

JOLENE BONTRAGER, Topeka, IN

Rice Sauce

2 cups mayonnaise
½ cup ketchup
3 tablespoons sugar
1 tablespoon garlic powder
1 tablespoon paprika

1 teaspoon salt
1 teaspoon onion powder
¼ teaspoon cayenne pepper
½ cup water

Mix together and store in refrigerator. Delicious served with rice.

MABEL YODER, Mount Vernon, OH

Bacon Dressing

1½ cups Miracle Whip salad
 dressing
¼ cup corn syrup
¼ cup milk
¼ cup crumbled fried bacon

1 tablespoon finely chopped
 onion
¼ teaspoon pepper
1 tablespoon parsley flakes

Stir all together until well blended. Refrigerate. Yield: 2½ cups.

MRS. VELMA SCHROCK, Goshen, IN

Sadie's Salad Dressing

3 cups mayonnaise
¼ cup prepared mustard
1 teaspoon celery seed
1½ cups sugar
½ cup vinegar

½ cup oil
1 teaspoon onion salt
2 teaspoons cucumber dill
  dip mix (optional)

Mix together with blender or whisk. Great on salads.

Mrs. Abner (Sadie) Fisher, Aaronsburg, PA

Salad Dressing

1 egg, plus enough water to
  fill ½ cup
¾ cup vegetable oil
½ teaspoon dry mustard
⅔ cup sugar

2 teaspoons salt
1 tablespoon lemon juice
1¼ cups water
⅓ cup Perma-Flo
½ cup vinegar

In large 3- to 4-quart bowl, beat together egg, oil, mustard, sugar, salt, and lemon juice. In saucepan, bring water to a boil. In small bowl, combine Perma-Flo and vinegar. Add to boiling water. Add this mixture to first mixture, beating very well with wire whisk. Good to use with most salads.

Mrs. Daniel Hershberger, Chili, WI

Homemade Cream Soup

3 tablespoons butter,
melted
3 tablespoons flour
¼ teaspoon salt
1 cup milk

Optional Additions (1 to
2 cups total): cheese,
chopped celery, chopped
onion, diced mushrooms,
etc.

Mix all together in saucepan and cook until thickened. Use in place of 1 can condensed cream soup.

MARY PETERSHEIM, Apple Creek, OH

Pork Sausage

8 ounces coarsely ground
pork sausage
2 tablespoons salt
½ cup diced hot peppers
1 tablespoon red pepper
3 pounds brown sugar

1 pound Tender Quick
1 heaping tablespoon
rubbed sage
1 heaping tablespoon dry
mustard
1 heaping tablespoon ginger

Mix all ingredients and grind together.

SARAH BEILER, Doylesburg, PA

Canned Walnuts

Put nut meats in jars with 2-piece lids. Place in 250-degree oven directly on rack for 45 minutes. Turn off oven and allow to cool before removing. Nuts will keep for several months.

ELIZABETH BYLER, New Wilmington, PA

Household

HOMEMADE PEDIALYTE

4 cups water
4 tablespoons sugar
1 cup orange juice

1 teaspoon baking soda
¼ teaspoon salt

Mix well and store in refrigerator for about 1 week. This is good for upset stomach or dehydration.

ANNA BYLER, Spartansburg, PA

COUGH SYRUP FOR WHOOPING COUGH

1 lemon, thinly sliced
½ pint flaxseeds

1 quart water
2 ounces honey

In saucepan, simmer lemon, flaxseeds, and water for 4 hours. Do not boil. Strain while hot and add honey. Pour into pint jar and fill with water.

Use as soon as cough is noticeable. Dose 1 tablespoon four times per day. Add an additional dose after each severe fit of coughing. This remedy has never failed me, bringing about a cure in 4 to 5 days.

EMME D. BYLER, New Wilmington, PA

DEEP CUTS

For a deep cut that keeps bleeding, put cayenne pepper on the cut and the bleeding will soon quit. Also helps the cut heal faster. Works well on our horses.

SUSAN BONTRAGER, Lagrange, IN

Fruit and Veggie Wash

½ cup apple cider vinegar   ½ cup water
½ cup lemon juice

Add ingredients to spray bottle and shake to combine. To use: spray liberally on fruits and vegetables, then rinse with cold water and prepare as usual. To store: refrigerate for up to 1 month.

Note: It is important to wash pesticides and germs off your produce. This solution removes residues and has germ-killing properties.

Sarah Esh, Kinzers, PA

Homemade Baby Wipes

1 roll heavy paper towels
1 cup water

2 capfuls rubbing alcohol
1 teaspoon baby wash

Cut paper towels in half. Fold up and put in container. Combine water, alcohol, and baby wash. Pour over towels. Put on lid and turn upside down until towels absorb liquid.

Clara A. Yoder, Sugar Grove, PA

Homemade Mild Sink Soap

Mix together ½ cup Dawn dish soap and 2 cups vinegar in spray bottle. Shake well before each use. We like this better than the brand-name versions. This is not as harsh and works great.

Susan Bontrager, Lagrange, IN

Liquid Soap

2½ gallons rainwater
1¾ cups lye
1 cup ammonia

2 cups liquid detergent
(I like Gain)
1 cup powdered detergent
(I like Gain)

Fill 5-gallon pail half full of cold rainwater. Add lye, ammonia, liquid detergent, and powdered detergent. Stir to dissolve, about 15 minutes. Let sit 30 minutes, then stir well. Fill bucket with water and stir thoroughly. Can leave in bucket with lid or store in bottles. Keep stirring soap as you dip it out as it will settle. Always stir or shake before using. Can be used for laundry, walls, ceiling, floors, furniture, etc.

Amanda Byler, Curwensville, PA

Window Cleaner

1 cup vinegar
10 to 15 drops lemon essential oil
Distilled water

Put vinegar and lemon oil in 1-quart container and fill with distilled water.

REGINA BONTRAGER, Lagrange, IN

Homemade Potpourri

1½ cups dried orange rind
1½ cups dried apple peel
1½ cups dried lemon rind

1 tablespoon whole allspice
3 tablespoons whole cloves
2 small star anise (optional)

Mix all and store in jar. Use a spoonful or two in a saucepan of water on low heat. Makes the house smell good.

RUBY MILLER, Auburn, KY

CHICKADEE PUDDING

1½ cups melted suet or
  cooking grease
1 cup breadcrumbs
1 cup cornmeal

½ cup sugar
2 tablespoons peanut butter
Sunflower seeds
Bird seed

Melt suet. Add breadcrumbs, cornmeal, sugar, and peanut butter. Stir in seeds. Pack in paper cups that can be easily removed once mixture hardens. Put in mesh bag and hang out for birds.

FEENIE BEILER, Delta, PA

All-Natural Insect Repellent

1 cup witch hazel
1 cup distilled water or aloe
vera juice
15 drops lemongrass
essential oil
10 drops eucalyptus
essential oil

10 drops citronella
essential oil
10 drops tea tree
essential oil
5 drops lavender
essential oil
5 drops cedarwood
essential oil

Mix all together in spray bottle. Shake well before each use. Apply every 2 to 3 hours to repel insects.

Note: avoid eye contact and broken skin.

SARAH ESH, Kinzers, PA

Plant Food

1 teaspoon baking powder
1 teaspoon Epsom salt
1 teaspoon saltpeter

½ teaspoon ammonia
1 gallon water

Mix together. Water plants every 5 to 6 days. Try it on your African violets and watch them bloom.

ANNA BYLER, Spartansburg, PA

Weed-Be-Gone

1 gallon vinegar
2 cups Epsom salt

¼ cup original Dawn dish
soap

Mix ingredients in spray bottle. Spray weeds in morning after dew has evaporated. Weeds should be dead by evening.

BETTY MILLER, Decatur, IN

COMMON EQUIVALENTS AND SUBSTITUTIONS

COMMON EQUIVALENTS

APPLES, 1 pound = about 3 medium

BEANS, 1 cup dry = 2 to 2½ cups cooked

BUTTER, 1 stick = 8 tablespoons or 4 ounces

CARROT, 1 medium = ½ cup chopped, shredded, or sliced

CHEESE, 4 ounces = 1 cup shredded

CHOCOLATE CHIPS, 6 ounces = 1 cup

EGG WHITE, 1 large = about 2 tablespoons

EGG YOLK, 1 large = about 1½ tablespoons

GELATIN, 1 envelope unflavored = 2½ teaspoons

GRAHAM CRACKERS, 1 cup crumbs = 7 whole crackers

HEAVY CREAM, 1 cup = 1¾ to 2 cups whipped cream

LEMON, 1 medium = 2 teaspoons zest and 3 tablespoons juice

LIME, 1 medium = 1½ teaspoons zest and 2 tablespoons juice

MUSHROOMS, 8 ounces = 3 cups chopped or sliced

ONION, 1 medium = ½ cup chopped

ORANGE, 1 medium = 1 tablespoon zest and ⅓ cup juice

PEPPER, BELL, 1 medium = ¾ cup chopped

POPCORN, ¼ cup unpopped = about 4 cups popped

POTATOES, 1 pound = about 3 medium, or 2¾ cups peeled and cubed, or 2 cups mashed

RICE, 1 cup uncooked = 3 cups cooked

TOMATO, 1 medium = ½ cup peeled, seeded, and chopped

Common Substitutions

BAKING POWDER, 1 teaspoon = ½ teaspoon cream of tartar plus ¼ teaspoon baking soda

BAKING SODA, 1 teaspoon = 4 teaspoons baking powder

BREADCRUMBS, DRY, ¼ cup = ¼ cup cracker crumbs OR ¼ cup cornflake crumbs OR 1 cup ground oats

BROTH, 1 cup = 1 teaspoon or 1 cube instant beef or chicken bouillon plus 1 cup hot water

BUTTER, 1 cup = 1 cup margarine OR 1 cup shortening or lard plus ¼ teaspoon salt

BUTTERMILK, 1 cup = 1 tablespoon lemon juice or vinegar plus enough milk to make 1 cup (let stand 5 minutes before using) OR ⅔ cup plain yogurt plus ⅓ cup water OR ½ cup plain yogurt or sour cream plus ½ cup milk

CHOCOLATE, unsweetened, 1 ounce = 3 tablespoons unsweetened cocoa powder plus 1 tablespoon oil or melted shortening

CORNSTARCH, 1 teaspoon = 1 tablespoon flour OR 1 teaspoon arrowroot starch

CORN SYRUP, 1 cup = 1¼ cups sugar plus ⅓ cup water OR 1 cup honey

CREAM CHEESE, 1 cup = 1 cup pureed cottage cheese OR 1 cup plain yogurt, strained overnight through cheesecloth

CREAM OF TARTAR, 1 teaspoon = 2 teaspoons lemon juice or vinegar

GARLIC, 1 clove = ½ teaspoon minced bottled garlic OR ⅛ teaspoon garlic powder

HALF-AND-HALF OR LIGHT CREAM, 1 cup = 1 tablespoon melted butter plus enough whole milk to make 1 cup OR 1 tablespoon water plus enough heavy cream to make 1 cup

HEAVY CREAM, 1 cup = ¾ cup milk plus ¼ cup melted butter (Note: will not whip)

Herbs, fresh, 1 tablespoon = $\frac{1}{2}$ to 1 teaspoon dried herb OR $\frac{1}{2}$ teaspoon ground herb

Honey, 1 cup = $1\frac{1}{4}$ cups sugar plus $\frac{1}{3}$ cup water OR 1 cup corn syrup

Ketchup, 1 cup = $\frac{1}{2}$ cup tomato sauce, 2 tablespoons sugar, 1 tablespoon vinegar, and 1 teaspoon ground cloves

Lard, 1 cup = 1 cup shortening or butter

Lemon juice, 1 teaspoon = $\frac{1}{2}$ teaspoon vinegar OR 1 teaspoon lime juice

Mayonnaise, 1 cup = 1 cup sour cream or plain yogurt

Milk, dairy, 1 cup = 1 cup light coconut, almond, or soy milk OR $\frac{2}{3}$ cup evaporated milk plus $\frac{1}{3}$ cup water OR $\frac{1}{2}$ cup heavy cream and $\frac{1}{2}$ cup water OR $\frac{1}{4}$ cup dry milk powder plus 1 cup water

Molasses, 1 cup = 1 cup honey OR $\frac{3}{4}$ cup brown sugar plus 1 teaspoon cream of tartar

Mustard, dry, 1 teaspoon = 1 tablespoon prepared mustard

Mustard, prepared, 1 tablespoon = 1 tablespoon dry mustard, 1 teaspoon vinegar, 1 teaspoon water, and 1 teaspoon sugar

Onion, chopped, $\frac{1}{2}$ cup = 2 tablespoons dry minced onion OR $\frac{1}{2}$ teaspoon onion powder

Perma-Flo starch, 1 tablespoon = 1 tablespoon arrowroot, cornstarch, Clear Jel, or Therm-flo OR 3 tablespoons flour

Shortening, 1 cup = 1 cup lard or butter

Sour cream, 1 cup = 1 cup plain yogurt

Sour milk, 1 cup = 1 tablespoon vinegar plus enough milk to make 1 cup

Soy sauce, $\frac{1}{2}$ cup = $\frac{1}{4}$ cup Worcestershire sauce plus 1 tablespoon water

Sugar, brown, 1 cup packed = 1 cup sugar plus 2 tablespoons molasses

Sugar, white, 1 cup = 1 cup packed light brown sugar OR 2 cups sifted powdered sugar

SWEETENED CONDENSED MILK, 1 (14 ounce) can = $\frac{3}{4}$ cup sugar plus $\frac{1}{2}$ cup water and $1\frac{1}{8}$ cup dry powdered milk; bring to a boil and cook about 20 minutes, stirring often, until thickened

TOMATO JUICE, 1 cup = $\frac{1}{2}$ cup tomato sauce plus $\frac{1}{2}$ cup water

TOMATO SAUCE, 2 cups = $\frac{3}{4}$ cup tomato paste plus 1 cup water

VANILLA BEAN, 1 whole = 2 teaspoons vanilla extract

VEGETABLE OIL FOR BAKING, 1 cup = 1 cup applesauce

VINEGAR, 1 teaspoon = 1 teaspoon lemon juice

Index of Contributors

Index of Recipes by Section

Breakfast

Beverages

Breads, Rolls, and Crackers

Salads and Side Dishes

Main Dishes

Desserts

Bars and Cookies

MISCELLANEOUS THINGS

HOUSEHOLD

Index of Recipes by Key Ingredients